Lives and Times

THE STATE HOUSE GARDEN, PHILADELPHIA

Lives and Times

Four Informal American Biographies

Stephen Jumel, Merchant
William Eaton, Hero
Theodosia Burr, Prodigy
Edmond Charles Genêt, Citizen

By

Meade Minnigerode

*" . . . I vaguely know
There were heroes of old,
Troubles more than the heart could hold . . ."*

VACHEL LINDSAY.

Illustrated

Essay Index Reprint Series

 BOOKS FOR LIBRARIES PRESS
FREEPORT, NEW YORK

First Published 1925
Reprinted 1970

INTERNATIONAL STANDARD BOOK NUMBER:
0-8369-1765-0

LIBRARY OF CONGRESS CATALOG CARD NUMBER:
76-121490

PRINTED IN THE UNITED STATES OF AMERICA

To

KNIGHT CHENEY COWLES

CONTENTS

PAGE

I.—STEPHEN JUMEL, MERCHANT 1

II.—WILLIAM EATON, HERO 51

III.—THEODOSIA BURR, PRODIGY 97

IV.—EDMOND CHARLES GENÊT, CITIZEN . . . 151

ILLUSTRATIONS

FACING
PAGE

THE STATE HOUSE GARDEN, PHILADELPHIA

Frontispiece

BETSY BOWEN DELACROIX 8
By St.-Mémin.

THE JUMEL MANSION 16

THE TONTINE COFFEE HOUSE, NEW YORK CITY . 32

WALL STREET AND THE BOWLING GREEN, NEW YORK
CITY 40

GENERAL WILLIAM EATON 56

BURNING OF THE U. S. FRIGATE *Philadelphia* IN THE
HARBOR OF TRIPOLI 64

GENERAL EATON AND HAMET BASHAW ON THE MARCH
TO DERNE 80

THEODOSIA BURR 100
By St.-Mémin.

JOSEPH BRANT 108
From the *London Magazine*, July, 1776.

THEODOSIA BURR ALSTON 124
By Vanderlyn.

FACING
PAGE

BLENNERHASSETT ISLAND 140

EDMOND CHARLES GENÊT 154

THE BATTERY, NEW YORK CITY, WITH THE FRIGATE
Embuscade 162
By Drayton, 1793.

THOMAS JEFFERSON 178
Original in the possession of the New York Historical Society.
Unfinished water-color sketch by Robert Field.

THE GOVERNMENT HOUSE, NEW YORK CITY . . 186

I

Stephen Jumel, Merchant

STEPHEN JUMEL, MERCHANT

I

STEPHEN JUMEL—of Stone, Liberty and Whitehall
Streets at New York—was, like his friend and French
fellow-countryman John Juhel, an importer of wines,
brandies, cordials, spirits, gins and other "choice
fluids."

At his emporium on Stone, and afterwards on
Liberty Street—his home was on Whitehall—one
found, in the early years of the last century, every
variety of Madeira, Teneriffe and Malaga, Jamaica,
Antigua and St. Croix, Holland rum and York
Anchor, All Fours, Metheglin, Aqua Mirable, Ladies'
Comfort and double distilled Life of Man. They
came, from England and Ireland, from France,
Portugal and Spain, from the Canaries and from the
West Indies, in kegs, puncheons and pipes, aboard
his brig, the *Stephen*, and his barque *Eliza*.

He was, in 1800, one of the wealthiest merchants
in the port of New York, although he had arrived
there practically penniless only a few years before;
an influential member, no doubt, of the Merchants'
Exchange, in the Tontine Coffee House on the corner
of Wall and Water Streets, where one might board

3

and lodge at ten shillings a day, and where the books were kept for entering and clearing vessels; and he possessed an elegant, two-storied, yellow brick mansion with dormer windows on the corner of Whitehall and Pearl, in the most fashionably aristocratic residential district in the city—although some were beginning to prefer State Street. There were dead cats, and live pigs, and mud in the street, and Pearl was so narrow that pedestrians going north were given the right of way over those going south, but through the doorways of the neighboring houses the whole social world of New York passed back and forth in flowered callimancoes, and in tight breeches and boots.

He knew the Livingstons, and the Clintons, and perhaps their lately naturalized son-in-law, Citizen Edmond Genêt; the Schuylers, the Jays and the Morrises, General Alexander Hamilton of the Grange and Colonel Aaron Burr of Richmond Hill; and the great merchants. Mr. John Jacob Astor who was always talking about furs and accumulating real estate, and Mr. Archibald Gracie who failed in 1812 because of the orders in council, and Mr. Robert Lenox who did not; the members of LeRoy, Bayard and Company, a firm already ten years old in 1800 and the most important counting house in the city, doing an enormous business with Europe and the West Indies; and Mr. Jacob Barker who owned more ships than anyone else in America—except Mr. William Gray with his fleet of thirty running out of Salem—and traded all over the seven seas from Russia, around both Capes, to China.

Jumel may not, as a foreigner, have taken a very active part in American politics, or have gone about wearing partisan cockades in his hat; but he had suffered from the consequences of the French Revolution, and was a great admirer of Mr. George Washington, so that he must have been welcome in the Federalist circles of the town—the "well born," "monarchist," Tory circles of the town which so annoyed Mr. Jefferson, and Mr. Brockholst Livingston, and the Republicans in general, in whose estimation Mr. Washington was only a dangerous hypocrite who longed to make himself king, and all Federalists tyrants, Anglomaniacs and betrayers of national liberty. Jumel was a supporter, probably, of the Bank, of neutrality in European affairs, and of Mr. Jay's commercial treaty with England; not to be enlisted by the beautiful, sparkling and otherwise irresistible Miss Theodosia Burr in the ranks of the Tenth Legion, or "Burr's Myrmidons" as General Hamilton called them; a reader of the *United States Gazette*, and not of Mr. Benjamin Franklin Bache's *Aurora*, in which startlingly scurrilous sheet "Lightning Rod Junior" saw fit to greet Mr. Washington's retirement from the Presidency with the following disparaging paragraphs—

"If ever a nation was debauched by a man, the American nation has been debauched by Washington. If ever a nation was deceived by a man, the American nation has been deceived by Washington. Let his example then be an example to future ages; let it serve to be a warning that no man may be an idol; let the history of the Federal Government instruct mankind that the mask of patriotism may be worn to conceal the fondest designs against the liberties of the people. . . .

"The man who is the source of all the misfortunes of our country is this day reduced to a level with his fellow citizens and is no longer possessed of power to multiply evils upon the United States. If ever there was a period for rejoicing this is the moment. Every heart, in unison with the freedom and happiness of the people, ought to beat high with exultation that the name of Washington ceases from this day to give currency to political iniquity and to legalize corruption."

Mr. Washington, it seems, was not popular in certain circles, with his gilded coach covered with cupids, and his yellow gloves, and his state sword in its white velvet scabbard. . . .

Personally, Jumel was a big man. Big physically, noted for his tall, broad chested, muscular stature; a handsome, graceful giant who danced divinely at the City Hotel Assemblies. Large minded, notorious for the farseeing wisdom of his mercantile operations. Great hearted, generous, impulsive, a man of wide sympathies and spontaneous charities—although it is not necessary here to repeat the well used anecdote of the cartman and the ten dollar piece—a kind, loyal and perhaps rather erratic soul.

One imagines him a trifle boisterous, quite conspicuous always, a good deal of an elephant at the ball, a practical joker probably; pleasantly Gallic in his humor, a terror with the ladies who undoubtedly adored him, an "uncle" to many neighboring children although he was never to be the father of any,

a gentleman who served on committees and to whom
one invariably went first for subscriptions, under
whose feet the earth shook when he laughed. A
little sensitive, a little proud, a little quick tempered.
A little hasty sometimes, and not always as wise as
he was good. A shrewd man who, caught in the
wrong mood by the right person, could be monumen-
tally imposed upon.

Cultured and well mannered, refined in his tastes—
these attributes had not yet become platitudes in his
day—prosperous, prominent and popular, for a few
years Stephen Jumel enjoyed the friendship, the
hospitality and the social amenities of his adopted
city—and then he made the indiscreet mistake of
purchasing a private carriage for a lady. . . .

2

Jumel had come to New York, in about 1795 it
seems, from Santo Domingo—via St. Helena. A
roundabout route, forced upon him by the fact that
he was not in a position to select the destination of
the ship in which he left the former island, since she
picked him up, a fugitive on the beach, with her own
sails already set for that other cheerless isolation in
the South Atlantic. There cannot have been many
ships following such a course, and it was unfortunate
for Jumel that he should have chanced upon that
particular, and one imagines exceptional, vessel; but
he was only too grateful to find himself on her deck,
bound for any port in the world outside of Santo
Domingo, for behind him an entire province was
burning, streaming with blood, roaring with slaves

risen against the white plantation owners under the
banner of Toussaint—that Congo chieftain's son
who so annoyed Napoleon finally that he condescend-
ed to insult him by calling him the Gilded African,
and honored him at the last with death in a mountain
fortress of the Jura, where there were no palm trees,
but only mists and snows.

It may have been in 1792, or perhaps in 1791, for
only a few months intervened between the two in-
surrections. Nor is it apparent now at what date
Jumel originally went out to Santo Domingo from
France, or whether possibly he was born on the island,
at one of the great plantations, at Limbé, or at the
Cape, or perhaps at Jacmel. At all events, he
came of good family, with influential connections in
France, and he had already made a fortune in the
Colony.

The French western province of Santo Domingo—
the name applied then to the entire island—the jewel
of the French West Indies, beside which, in 1790,
Guadaloupe and delightfully wicked Martinique
were only minor brilliants. A colony claiming the
greater part of the mother country's commercial
attention, with its extensive production of coffee,
sugar, cotton and indigo. A colony of six hundred
thousand souls, five hundred thousand of whom were
full blooded Congo slaves, some sixty thousand free
mulattoes and the remainder French creoles in
whom were vested all social and political privileges.
And among these varied thousands, a few hundred
planters and officials from France, with their families;
people who came and went on the packets from

BETSY BOWEN DELACROIX
By St. Memin

Nantes, and sent their children home to convent and monastery schools. People like Stephen Jumel. The aristocracy of queenly Santo Domingo.

For these life was passing, pleasantly and lazily, but very prosperously, and extremely decorously, on the great plantations—such as that on which a lad called Toussaint was learning to read a little under his master's care—a white family here, a white family there, the planter and his womenfolk, boys, girls, babies, surrounded by thousands of slaves. A serene existence, securely established in a rigorous tradition of castes. And then, in 1790, a ship brought the startling news from France that all men were equal, and that aristocracy was not an essential feature of social organization. There was considerable repetition of the words Liberty, Equality and Fraternity. The words, and the idea, were novel in Santo Domingo and appealed at once as excellent ones to the mulattoes, who forthwith claimed equality of rights with their French fellow-colonists. The National Assembly at Paris, when referred to, knowing less than nothing of social conditions in Santo Domingo, gave its distant approbation to these demands and returned to its speech making. The creoles in the colony immediately espoused the royalist cause, determined to ignore this, to them, fatal decree of the republican Assembly. Civil strife was imminent between the sixty thousand mulattoes and the forty thousand creoles, when suddenly, in August, 1791—and presumably the well meaning National Assembly had not foreseen this consequence of its wholesale and undiluted promulgation of unaccustomed liberty—the five hundred thousand slaves revolted.

3

The insurrection broke out first on one of the plantations near the Cape. There, a slave was seen, in the early evening, running from a shed to which he had apparently just set fire. The subsequent morning brought news from other localities of similar manifestations of insubordination and disquiet, the sudden, forerunning gusts of the tempest which was, in a few hours, to sweep the province. On one plantation the slaves had spent the night dancing around a fire.

Dancing around a fire.

One begins to sense the precarious uncertainty of life in the Colony, the constant shadow darkening the background of all daily intercourse, when so trivial a circumstance, so pleasant a domestic spectacle as that of a parcel of slaves dancing around a fire, must be considered a cause of alarm and necessitate the sending abroad of anxious messengers.

One would like to know how long already they had been dancing around hidden fires in the jungle, listening to old Congo war chants, shivering under a pale moon at the ritual of voodoo priests, while the maddening drum beats went booming through the night. One would like to appreciate the cunning, the deception, the silent network of preparation, the genius and inspiration, the accumulated inheritance of hatred and the fantastic hopes, the tribal memories and aspirations behind it all. One would like to have a glimpse of this spiritual return to ancient Africa there in distant Santo Domingo.

Unfortunately one sees only the relapse into hot blooded savagery which followed; one is made aware only of the fanatic cruelties, the ritualistic atrocities, the ferocious vengeances unchained; one learns only of grim dances around torturing fires, of ghastly ceremonies before tribal altars, of unthinkable physical horrors committed in the terrifying presence of unspeakable banners. One reads, in the report of the Commissioners from Santo Domingo to the French Assembly—which did not appear especially moved —of living bodies encased in planks and then sawed in two; of babies carried on pikes at the head of demented processions; of frenzied orgies which transcend imagination. One reads other sickening paragraphs.

But in the midst of it all one is obliged to remember two things—that the same treatment was accorded those slaves themselves, and there were many who refused to join the insurrection and remained superbly loyal to their masters; and that there was scarcely an instance of fiendishly depraved cruelty in the uprising of the slaves of Santo Domingo which cannot be duplicated, if not actually surpassed, in the scenes of popular insanity which attended the Reign of Terror in the civilized cities of France. When one thinks of Santo Domingo one must not forget Paris and her prison massacres, or Lyons and her "republican marriages," or Nantes and her "national bath." And when one thinks of the slave leaders of the insurrection one must not forget Carrier and Fouquier-Tinville, Marat and Robespierre.

One would do well, in fact, to remember Philadelphia, where, at a slightly later date, earnest and pathetically ridiculous American "republican" patriots gathered annually at banquets for the purpose of commemorating the execution of Louis XVI—at which solemn and undeniably civilized functions otherwise intelligent citizens plunged carving knives into the body of an emblematic pig and quaffed its blood in execration of the "tyrant"; self respecting, Christian citizens of Philadelphia, who danced in a ring afterwards around the table wearing red liberty caps, very far removed no doubt from Toussaint and his Congo rabbles.

The insurrection, originating near Limbé and the Cape, and centering its utmost violence and destruction in the regions of Port Margot, Petite Anse and the Grand Ravine of Limbé, spread throughout the Province. Plantations, factories, warehouses, cane fields, the torch was put to everything. Entire families were driven from their homes, tracked to their places of panic-stricken refuge and butchered. The Northern Plain was a blood-stained desolation of flaming ruins. In November, Port-au-Prince itself was burned.

Those colonists who escaped immediate massacre found themselves fugitives in a land wasted by fire and sword, distracted wanderers—men, women and little children—through a hostile countryside, terrified, fever smitten, starving and destitute. The more fortunate ones managed to reach the Cape and the protection of its garrison. Others succeeded in passing over the border into the Spanish province

where, at least, there was security from the night-
mare. Others, again, sought hiding places in the
forests and jungles, where they were hunted down
relentlessly by the pursuing bands, or else met the
more merciful end afforded by hunger, and thirst,
and sickness. A few came stumbling out at last
upon forlorn beaches—tattered, emaciated human
remnants scanning an empty horizon, or lumbering
with pitiful cries and imploring gestures through the
sand after some passing ship. Among these was
Stephen Jumel.

On what beach, or in what company, and after
what vicissitudes is not known now. Always robust
and valiant, he may not have suffered as much as
most. One does not know, either, how long he
waited on that beach, whether many ships passed
tantalizingly beyond his reach, or whether the first
was the one to send her boat to rescue him, attracted
by his frantic signals. At all events, she took him
aboard and carried him to St. Helena, her first port
of call. There he left her, to await a vessel returning to America or, possibly, to Europe. He landed,
eventually, at New York where his former business
connections held out some hope of financial rehabili-
tation.

4

It was a funny little town when Jumel first came
to it.

Approached from the Bay—filled with snows,
brigs, schooners and polaccas, British frigates with
blue upper works and French ones carrying red

Liberty caps at the mastheads, Albany sloops bearing timber, skins and grain to exchange for tammies,
broadcloths and halfthicks, and two masted periaguas
ferrying back and forth between Brooklyn or Paulus
Hook and the city wharves—the most conspicuous
feature of the waterfront to attract the visitor's
attention, the combined Riverside Drive and Central
Park of that day, was the Battery.

A public walk along the water's edge surmounted
by a battery of thirteen guns placed *en barbette* on a
stone platform, behind which rose a truncated stone
tower topped by a flagstaff with a golden ball, popu-
larly referred to as the Churn.   The remaining space
between these fortifications and the Government
House, on the site of the old Fort George and of the
future Custom House, was occupied by terraces and
walks, shaded by elm trees, along which the entire
population took its ease in the cool of the day.   In
front of Government House, a little way back from
the Battery gardens, stood an elliptical plot of grass
still spoken of as the Bowling Green, and containing
the crumbling pedestal of what had once been a
statue of King George.   There Broadway began, a
fine, wide thoroughfare not yet come into its own as
a residential avenue, straggling past the Common
with its gibbet, and dwindling soon into a country
road leading towards Lispenard's meadows, where
one went duck shooting and berry gathering.

On the other side of the Common, destined to be
known in time as City Hall Park, was Chatham
Street, from which the carts started every morning
to distribute the water taken from the Tea Water

Pump—for New York could not boast of a system of wooden water pipes such as served the metropolis of Philadelphia. And from Chatham Street one went to Boston, through the Bowery Lane, halting to pick up passengers for the Boston and Albany stage at the Bull's Head Tavern, which Mr. Richard Varian conducted on the property owned by a prosperous butcher of the Fly Market called Henry Ashdor, or, as some people pronounced it, Astor. Or one followed the continuation of the Bowery Lane and went to Kingsbridge through McGowan's Pass. Or, at the junction of the Bowery and Monument Lanes, one turned down the latter and went to the village of Greenwich, two miles distant, stopping perhaps at Brannan's Tea Gardens to consume iced liquors and creams and visit the aloes and orange trees in the greenhouse.

A pretty place, Greenwich, just beyond the Minetta Brook to the north of Lispenard's meadows; noted for its salubrious climate, a refuge in time of pestilence, adorned with handsome residences set among its wooded hills; and crowned by Colonel Burr's great porticoed mansion of Richmond Hill, where a plump, rosy little girl of twelve called Theodosia sat at the head of the table and dispensed her widowed father's lavish hospitality with all the grace and self assurance of a grown woman of the world.

Brook, meadows and wooded hills, they have all vanished now, and so also has Bayard's Mount, over to the eastward, a landmark of New York in Jumel's time. Bayard's Mount, or Bunker Hill,

situated at the spot where now Mulberry Street
brings its traffic to Grand, incredulous of the emi-
nence which once overlooked the surrounding countryside, the highest point near the city, on which,
in 1798, Mr. Joseph Delacroix opened his popular
resort called the Vauxhall Garden, for the enjoyment of illuminations, fireworks and modest refresh-
ments.

And with Bayard's Mount another landmark well
known to Jumel has disappeared—the Fresh Water
Pond, or Collect, a sheet of water in which one fished
and upon which one skated, where now the Tombs
prison stands, stonily unconscious of these forgotten
amenities.   Jumel saw it filled in, along in 1808, by
order of the City Council which had lost patience
with a population which persisted in throwing refuse
into it; and, already in 1800, he had watched the
stream which served as its outlet to the Hudson
through Lispenard's meadows straightened and deep-
ened, and furnished with a roadway on either side,
so that people began to speak of it as the "Canal
Street."

A little later Jumel probably joined his fellow
citizens in ridiculing the vestry of Trinity Church
when it saw fit to invade that desolate region of
brambles and marshes just south of the canal and
west of Broadway, and proceed with the erection of
a church which was promptly dubbed St. John's-in-
the-Fields, and with the laying out of a park which
it proposed to call St. John's Park.   And having
laughed at this folly, Jumel lived long enough to see
the Park becoming one of the most exclusive resi-

THE JUMEL MANSION

dential sections in the city; but in those earlier days it had not seemed likely that the town would ever reach so far to the west and north.

For the town, as Jumel first knew it, its residences and counting houses, its warehouses and shops, its taverns and gardens, and its wharves, all lay to the east of Broadway, from the Battery up to the Bowery Lane. There was no shipping to be found in the Hudson, almost no activity to take one west of Broadway, unless one were bound to Philadelphia by way of the ferry from Bussing's Wharf to Paulus Hook, or to Greenwich along the "shore road," the remains of which are now many blocks inland from the river front. One lived on Whitehall and State Streets, on Broad and Cherry Streets, in little red and yellow brick buildings; one did business on Stone and Pearl Streets, on Liberty, Wall and New, and on Piewoman's Lane which is now Nassau Street; one went shopping on Petticoat Lane, near White-hall, for amens and cordurets, for moreens, rattinetts and shalloons, for ribdelures, ticklenburghs, velverets and romals, and for putticals and setetersoys; on Water, Front and South Streets one found the chandlers and shipping offices, and the "cheap john" auctions, with bells, and red flags, and vendue masters.

And at Borden's Wharf and Constable's, at the Exchange, at the Coffee House, at the Old, and at Coenties Slips one found the ships themselves, bringing tea, and spice, and porcelain, camphor and silk from China, coffee, sugar and rum from Antigua and St. Kitts, from Jamaica, Guadaloupe and Mar-

tinique, and loading grain, leather and flour, and
quintals of fish.   There was a pleasant smell of tar
in the air, of aromatic cargoes piled up along the
sidewalks, of clean, fresh canvas in the sailmakers'
lofts; a constant clattering of blocks and tackles, of
mawls and hammers in the shipbuilding yards where
Mr. Cheesman, and Mr. Ackley, and Mr. Eckford
were so busy; the shiny hats and bright shirts of
many sailormen were in the streets, and a great
singing of deep water songs all along the docks.   One
made money, fabulously and decorously, and in the
evening one strolled gently along the Battery. . . .

5

A merchant himself, Jumel must have fitted in
very readily to the life of the town.   He made himself known, received introductions at the Tontine
Coffee House where all the business of the port was
transacted, looked up his former connections.   Perhaps he was given a desk for a while in some friendly
colleague's counting house.   He began to make
money.

Soon he must have been able to afford the seven
dollar a week luxury of Mrs. Loring's boarding house
at the foot of Broadway, or possibly that of Corré's
Hotel a little further up the street.   Or he may have
preferred the City Hotel, opposite Mr. Chenelette
Dusseaussoir's confectionery establishment, at that
time, and until the coming of the Astor House, the
finest and most pretentious hostelry in the country.
For his meals, if he chose to dine out in the middle
of the afternoon, he probably went to the Porter

House on Pine Street to enjoy Mr. Michael Little's renowned French cooking, or to Fraunces's when the latter became its landlord. Once in a while he may have gone to Mr. Dyde's London Hotel, next door to the Park Theater, for supper; or to Martling's Tavern on the corner of Nassau and George Streets, although after 1799, when the somewhat dilapidated structure which the Federalists called the Pig Pen had become the wigwam of the Tammany Society and consequently the great "republican" hangout, he may not have cared to be seen in its long room.

For recreation, when he grew tired of perusing *The Dessert to the True American* or *The Political Magazine and Miscellaneous Repository of Ballston, N. Y.*, he went and sat with his hat on in the pit of the Park Theater and got himself pelted with fruit, chop bones and empty bottles by the gods in the gallery; he inspected the mammoth's tooth, and the Chinese birds' nests, and the wampum belts in the Museum, and had his profile drawn by the physiognotrace; or else he patronized an itinerant show and looked at the automatons, and the musical clocks, and the electric "thunder houses," and the catoptric "penetrating spy glasses."

And in the spring and summer times he visited the gardens. The Mount Vernon where one rode on the flying horses, and the Columbian on State Street at which one stopped for an ice after walking on the Battery, Vauxhall on Bayard's Mount, and later on the Bowery Lane, where for fifty cents one watched the fireworks, and the balloons, and the acrobats, and listened to the music, and admired the large equestrian statue of Mr. Washington; and Contoit's which was an eminently respectable resort for ladies, where they might sit in little green compartments under the lamplit trees and consume vanilla ice cream, pound cake and lemonade for the modest sum of one shilling—although, it being a strictly temperance garden, wine negus and cognac were also to be obtained. Or else he hired a coachee and went out to the Belvidere Club on the East River, to see the view from the Captain's Walk and dine in the octagonal ballroom; or to Ranelagh near Corlaer's Hook, with its shady lawns; or up to the Indian Queen on the Boston Post Road.

Or else to Marriner's Tavern in Haarlem, which had once been the Roger Morris House, and which he was in time to rechristen the Jumel Mansion. . . .

6

In other respects, in a community in which the whole of civic life unfolded itself daily in the lobbies of the Tontine Coffee House, there was plenty to occupy Jumel's attention.

In the first place, for a number of almost uninterruptedly successive seasons, beginning in July and ending in November, there was the yellow fever. It came from the West Indies, found a congenial breeding place in the city's filth and carrion infested atmosphere and counted its victims by the hundreds, both at New York and at Philadelphia. It found a valuable ally, also, in the solemn imbecilities practiced by the prevailing schools of medicine in that era.

When, for instance, repeated blood lettings and administrations of clam juice were not found helpful to the patient, it was deemed salutary to burn pitch in his chamber, behind carefully closed windows, and to fire off horse pistols at his bedside. In the streets, one made bonfires, and the detonations of fowling pieces adding their din to the doleful clanging of all the church bells in town increased the sufferings of the sick who might otherwise have died peacefully of the fever alone. Those who were not stricken smeared themselves with Haarlem Oil and Vinegar of the Four Thieves, put garlic in their shoes, drenched their garments with balm of aloes, wore bags of camphor hung around their necks, and chewed enormous quids of tobacco. The more fortunate ones departed quietly to Greenwich, underwent a little prudent cupping and leeching, and dosed themselves with fantastic concoctions of rhubarb, senna and molasses.

And then there was politics, uproarious, frenzied, scurrilous, riot and duel provoking politics. Not the professional, carefully organized and consequently impersonal variety of a later day in which citizens have to be reminded for weeks at a time that if they do not register they cannot vote, so fundamentally negligent have they become in national affairs; but a tumultuous, breathless, almost apoplectic individual concern in each successive question of Governmental policy, which brought the entire town out into the streets on the slightest provocation to indulge in acrimonious debates enlivened by the most unseemly epithets, and settled, frequently, not by

the weight of arguments produced but by that of
cudgels raining on Federalist or Republican heads.
In fact, throughout the early years of Jumel's acquaintance with it, American history was a glorified
mob scene set to the frivolous music of indifferent
ballads.

And while, at least in the beginning, the underlying
causes of all this popular tumult cannot have been
of any immediate interest to Jumel, still the tumult
itself must have aroused his curiosity and caused
him considerable amusement. He must, for instance, have laughed very heartily at the pamphlet
entitled *A Bone to Gnaw for the Democrats*, in which
that inimitable Mr. "Peter Porcupine" remarked
that—

"In these toasting times it would have been something wonderful if the *sans culottes* in America had
neglected to celebrate the taking of Amsterdam by
their brethren in France. I believe from my soul
there have been more cannons fired here in the cele-
bration of this conquest than the French fired in
achieving it. I think I have counted twenty-two
grand civic festivals, fifty-one of an inferior order,
and one hundred and ninety-three public dinners.
. . ."

He may, indeed, have been genuinely alarmed by
those further paragraphs of "Porcupine's" in *The
Bloody Buoy thrown out as a warning to the Political
Pilots of America*, setting forth that—

"There is not a single action of the French revolutionists but has been justified and applauded in our
public papers, and many of them in our public

assemblies. Anarchy has its open advocates. We have seen the guillotine toasted to three times three cheers. And what would the reader say were I to tell him of a member of Congress who wished to see one of the murderous machines, employed for lopping off the heads of aristocrats, permanent in the State House yard of the City of Philadelphia?

"If these men of blood had once got the sword into their hands they would have mowed us down like stubble. We might have seen the banks of the Delaware, like those of the Loire, covered with human carcasses and its waters tinged with blood: ere this we might have seen our parents butchered, and even the head of our admired and beloved President rolling on the scaffold."

And, as a Frenchman who had himself suffered from the consequences of the French Revolution, he probably appreciated the justice of another statement in the same pamphlet, in which the writer pointed out that—

"Unfortunately for America, Great Britain has thrown from her the principles of the French revolutionists with indignation and abhorrence. This has served, in some measure, as a guide to our opinions and has been one of the principal motives for our actions. A combination of circumstances has so soured the minds of the great mass of the people in this country, has worked up their hatred against Great Britain to such a pitch, that the instant that nation is named they lose not only their temper but their reason also. Whatever the British adopt must be rejected, and whatever they reject must be adopted. Hence it is that all the execrable acts of the French legislators, not forgetting their murders and their blasphemy, have met with the most unqualified applauses, merely because they were execrated in the island of Britain."

For the whole subject of American foreign policy— and a considerable part of presidential, and consequently of state and city politics—was conditioned, during approximately the first decade at least of Jumel's sojourn at New York, upon a single criterion, that of French or English partisanship.

It is difficult in the present age of magnificent national isolation to appreciate that era, prior to the promulgation of Mr. Monroe's safeguarding doctrine, when America found herself constantly involved in Anglo-French affairs, much as a school of fish may be said to be involved in the net which surrounds them. The English had apparently not yet accustomed themselves to the fact that America was no longer a British colony, and persisted in their manifold interferences with American maritime commerce; the French, on the other hand, were rapidly convincing themselves that the resources and institutions of the sister republic were intended primarily for their use, and lost no opportunity of pointing out to the American people in what respects their Government fell short in its conception of this happy partnership; America viewed these two states of mind and sided vociferously against one or the other, stopping occasionally to send envoys plenipotentiary across the water, who, like Francis I, returned with very little else save honor. It is significant, perhaps, that the future author of the Monroe Doctrine was on several occasions a disgruntled member of these fruitless and exasperating embassies.

And it is difficult, in this day of sophisticated indifference to European crises, to appreciate the tremendous effect produced in America by the French Revolution, the fanatic enthusiasm or the passionate hostility, the mania of imitation or the phobia of repudiation, aroused throughout the greater portion of the United States by that transatlantic event.

One is apt to forget that Liberty poles surmounted by French Liberty Caps stood on many an American township green or public square; that Jacobin Clubs, patterned after those in France and in some cases affiliated with them, flourished in the large American cities and enrolled some of their most prominent citizens; that at Philadelphia, triumphal arches were erected to commemorate the execution of Louis XVI; that at Boston, people stopped playing omber and quadrille, and played instead a new game called Revolution, in which the king was known as Capet, the Queen as Strumpet and the Ace as La Guillotine; that from South Carolina to Maine the Democratic Societies were busy tearing down statues of kings, changing street names reminiscent of royalty and refusing to address anyone as "sir," or to sign any document "your humble servant"; and that at New York, where a beautiful, red silk Liberty Cap hung for many months in a place of honor on the wall at the Tontine Coffee House, men called each other "citizen" and their wives "citess," cut their hair in French style "à la Brutus" and adopted the utmost extremes of French fashion in dress. From one end of America to the other, *Yankee Doodle* was drowned out by the sounds of the *Marseillaise*, of the *Carmagnole* and of the *Ca Ira*.

7

Jumel came in time to observe many of these extravagances. In 1795, Citizen Edmond Genêt had only recently completed his triumphant journey from Charleston to Philadelphia, during the course of which he was received as a sort of itinerant apotheosis of Liberty, and given the Fraternal Hug by enormous concourses of American burghers. Only a little while before, Citizen Bompard of the French frigate *Embuscade* had defeated the British frigate *Boston* just outside Sandy Hook, and had been welcomed back to his anchorage in the East River by a deliriously jubilant population all decked out in tricolor cockades. Mr. Jay was but that moment returned from his mission to England for the purpose of negotiating a treaty of amity and commerce, and Jumel was very probably a spectator of that mass meeting in front of Federal Hall, at which twenty-eight reasons were found for condemning the shameful document, and Mr. Alexander Hamilton was stoned by the mob for presuming to defend it. Perhaps that evening Jumel listened to Republican supper parties toasting each other at the Indian Queen.

"A perpetual harvest to America! But clipped wings, lame legs, the pip and an empty crop to all Jays!"

"The Republic of America—may she never mistake jaybirds for eagles!"

Then in 1796, Jumel witnessed his first presidential campaign, and learned that Mr. Washington had only refused a third term because he knew that he could not be reëlected, and that he had warned the country against permanent alliances with any portion of the foreign world only because he had just made a treaty with England and did not wish Congress to make a similar one with France; aside from that, Mr. Washington was conceited, avaricious, hot tempered, unprincipled, an aristocrat and an anglomaniac, a person of low character, if the truth be told an embezzler, and more ostentatious than an eastern pashaw.

And Jumel learned also that Mr. John Adams hated the French Revolution, that he was a monarchist who hoped that his sons would succeed him on the throne of America, and that he had written a book in which he advocated a titled nobility to keep down the *canaille* multitudes. And as for Mr. Jefferson, Jumel learned that he was an infidel, that he denied that shells found on mountain tops were proof of the flood, that he maintained that the large bones found in the west were those of prehistoric animals called mammoths and not those of giants; that he was a philosopher, an inventor of whirligig chairs and, in fact, a mere college professor; and that he was a poltroon who never came out in the open against his adversaries but hired other people to write scurrilous lampoons against them. On the other hand, Mr. Jefferson was an ardent lover of

France, and he had no sons and so could not hope to see himself the founder of an American dynasty.

So, in that day, American presidential campaigns took their delightfully idiotic course, on a flood of spirited and highly libelous pamphlets signed by Camillus, and Brutus, and Cato.

And then, in 1798, the shoe was suddenly on the other foot. Mr. Pinckney, the American envoy at Paris, had been ordered out of France. Reinforced by Mr. John Marshall and Mr. Elbridge Gerry he had returned to Paris, only to become subjected by Citizen Talleyrand and the members of the Directoire to certain financial negotiations incompatible with the dignity of his mission, as a result of which someone in the American delegation was reported to have exclaimed—

"Millions for defense, not one cent for tribute!"

The slogan rang across the Atlantic and throughout the United States. America had been insulted, her envoys treated with contumely. The piratical activities of the French, directed against American shipping in the West Indies, were recalled. The pamphlets came fluttering from the presses—*The Cannibal's Progress*, *Sans Culotte Piracy*, *Dear Sister France*.

As a Frenchman, Jumel must have watched these events with apprehension; he would have had little sympathy for the France of Talleyrand and the Directoire, but France was always France, and the two countries were inevitably drifting into war. In vain the Republicans roared against the "war hawks," flaunted tricolor cockades, burned Mr. John Adams in effigy and sang—

> "See Johnny at the helm of state,
> Head itching for a crowny;
> He longs to be, like Georgy, great,
> And pull Tom Jeffer downy . . ."

The nation was aroused to a tremendous pitch of patriotic enthusiasm; everywhere, the Societies of Associated Youth were parading with black cockades in their hats—Washington's cockade, the Federal cockade, the *American* cockade—in the theaters, audiences stood on their seats to hear the President's March, and "Stony Point," and a recent one called "Hail Columbia." For once the *Marseillaise*, and the *Carmagnole*, and the *Ca Ira* were drowned out by a new version of *Yankee Doodle*—

> "Columbians all, the present hour
> As brothers should unite us;
> Union at home's the only way
> To make the nation right us.
>> Yankee Doodle, guard your coast,
>> Yankee Doodle Dandy.
>> Fear not, then, nor threat nor boast,
>> Yankee Doodle Dandy!
> Americans, then fly to arms,
> And learn the way to use them;
> If each man fights to defend his rights
> The French can't long abuse them.
>> Yankee Doodle—mind the tune—
>> Yankee Doodle Dandy,
>> If Frenchmen come we'll mind the tune,
>> And spank them hard and handy!"

And soon there was war, a little ghost of a war which never achieved the honor of official recognition in history, but which lasted for more than two years. Mr. Alexander Hamilton was appointed Major General; the merchants of New York—and perhaps Jumel among them, for i⁴ was the France of the Terror that America was fighting—subscribed thirty thousand dollars in one hour for the "rising navy"; on the sea, Truxton, Bainbridge and Porter, Hull, Rodgers and the two Decaturs wrote brilliant pages into the naval annals of America.

And in the midst of it all an incident took place which must have seemed of enormous importance to Jumel, and which may well have colored his whole future attitude towards American politics and made of him an ardent Republican, a supporter of Mr. Jefferson and of Colonel Burr, an advocate of the French party in America in spite of its admiration for the Revolution and the Terror. At all events, it may have laid the foundation for his subsequent devotion to Napoleon Bonaparte.

For in 1798, during the course of the French war, the American Government had suspended all relations with the French colonies in the West Indies. Realizing that this action meant starvation for Santo Domingo, Toussaint, who was now in power, declared his independence of France and begged the United States for a renewal of trade. The Renewing Act was consequently passed, in April, 1799, a Consul General was sent to the Cape, and an American squadron assisted Toussaint at the capture of Jacmel, as a result of which the leader of the slaves overcame the last remnant of French authority and made himself absolute master of the Colony.

One imagines Jumel stalking into the Tontine Coffee House in a fine fury on the day this news reached him, and reviling an administration which had seen fit to make common cause with the chief of the insurrection by placing its navy at his disposal, and signing treaties with the monster—for to Jumel the extraordinary Toussaint can never have been anything else. And as for Napoleon, one suspects that it was not the glamor of his name or the glories of his armies in Europe which so enthralled Jumel, but the fact that, in 1802, the First Consul sent an army of ten thousand men to Santo Domingo and carried off the Gilded African to imprisonment and miserable death, after as cold blooded a piece of treachery as ever darkened the record of human relations. But Jumel would not have cared about that. Later on, perhaps, towards the close of his own unfortunate life, but not then. It was sufficient that the black days and nights of the insurrection were at last avenged. . . .

8

And in the meantime, while all these turbulent events were taking place, there was living at New York a young lady who called herself Eliza Brown, who had already seen a good deal of the world, geographically and metaphorically, and who was destined to see even more of it.

It is with considerable diffidence that one ap-

proaches the history of this Miss Eliza Brown, so
contradictory is the information available concerning her earlier career, to say nothing of her parent-
age, and so well established now are the legends
which cling to her later and more respectable years.
It is, for instance, not without misgiving that one
finds oneself obliged to point out that the "gifted"
Madame Burr, the momentary partner of the aged
Vice-President in his second and somewhat incom-
prehensible matrimonial venture—that "cultured
lady of the world" who appears so alluringly in the
encyclopedias, the reputed friend of Lafayette,
Hamilton and Jefferson, of Louis Napoleon, and
of every other celebrity of her long day—seems in
reality to have been a person of no education or
breeding, sprung from the lowest origins, and considerably more restricted in her circle of fine ac-
quaintances than obituary literature would lead one
to believe.

One would like, indeed, to accept the obituary
pronouncement in its entirety, since truth is always
so much stranger, and frequently so much less flatter-
ing, than fiction. One might then accept the legend
of Madame Burr to be's birth, in 1769, in the cabin
of a French frigate carrying troops from Brest to
the West Indies, an event which caused the death of
her mother, an English lady called Capet—not a
common name in England, or even in France where
it happened to be that of the reigning family. There
is something extremely intriguing, in fact, about this
English lady called Capet, traveling in a French
frigate from Brest to the West Indies in 1769. One

THE TONTINE COFFEE HOUSE
New York City

would then continue to place credence in the legend
which drove the French frigate so far out of her
course that she found herself at Newport, Rhode
Island; thereby allowing the motherless baby called
Capet to be adopted by a certain charitable Mrs.
Thompson, from whose sheltering protection she
eloped to New York at the age of seventeen with an
English colonel called Peter Croix—pronounced
Crux, no doubt—on whose arm she entered upon the
brilliant career which was to bring her "into contact
with the best people in the city." One would like
very much to believe all that.

Overwhelmed, however, by the documentary and
legal evidence produced by such writers as Mr. W. H.
Shelton, the historian of the Jumel Mansion and of
its last eccentric chatelaine, one prefers to believe—
one is, in fact, obliged to believe—that Madame Burr
to be was born, not in the cabin of a French frigate
in 1769, but at Providence in 1775; the daughter of
a certain lady of slight social prominence called
Phebe Bowen, *née* Kelley, and of her husband John
Bowen, a mariner who got himself drowned in the
harbor of Newport; and that the child was named
Eliza, or Betsy, Bowen. There ensued nineteen
years of vagrant and altogether disreputable existence, during which Betsy, when she was not serving
terms in the workhouse, followed the itinerant fortunes of her mother and of the latter's successive
broods by varying husbands. Such culture and
refinement as she may have acquired during this
period remain highly problematical and nebulous.
She was known, on the other hand, as the hand-

somest girl in Providence, and in that verdict one must find her greatest gift and the secret of all her future success.

Finally, in 1794, when she was nineteen, Betsy, for apparently the only time in her life, took upon herself the dignity of motherhood without assuming any of its obligations. In the home of a Mistress Freelove Ballou—one would not presume to invent a name like that—she gave birth to a boy who was named George Washington Bowen, and who for many long years startled the inhabitants of Providence by the striking resemblance of his features to those of the Father of His Country. Betsy herself promptly abandoned the child and went to New York, not on the arm of Colonel Peter Croix, but on the New York and Providence packet.

During the next four obscure years she only appears once; as the wife, *de facto*, of Captain Jacques de la Croix—and there, probably, is the Colonel Peter Croix of the legend—a ship's captain who took her with him to France, and seems to have had her profile drawn by the famous Saint-Mémin, for she was then a widely known and acknowledged beauty. And then she became "separated" from her sea captain, one hears no more of Madame de la Croix, or of Betsy Bowen for that matter, and it is as Eliza Brown that one finds her living at New York in the last years of the century—a very beautiful young woman who had been across the Atlantic, perhaps several times, enough to cause her to be pointed at admiringly in the street in that untraveled age.

9

When was it that Jumel first saw Eliza Brown?
What was it in her that finally attracted him—her
beauty, of course, but perhaps also the fact that she
had been across the water, that she spoke a little of
his native tongue, that she was full of charming little
French ways that reminded him of home?

In any case, in 1800, Jumel took a step which may
have seemed natural enough from his foreign point
of view, but which threw the social world of New
York into a state of virtuously scandalized indignation.   Jumel had presumed to do publicly that which
decorum required should be kept private.   He in-
stalled Miss Eliza Brown in his mansion on Whitehall
Street, and went quietly about his business.   But
that was not all.   He bought her a carriage; not a
gilded coach, perhaps, all covered with cupids and
nymphs like Mr. Washington's, but a fine carriage
none the less, made by Mr. Abraham Quick on Broad
Street, in which the lady took pleasure in parading
her charms all up and down the length of New York's
most cherished residential quarter.   Her presence
there might in time have been condoned, that of her
carriage was an unpardonable offense to less fortunate
matrons who took their airings in hired vehicles, or,
many of them indeed, on foot.   Some things can
never be forgiven.   New York society turned its
back on Jumel; he was to reap the pitiless harvest
of his hot headed sowing in a long martyrdom of
ostracism.

For four years he waited, socially becalmed in his

great mansion on Whitehall Street, and then, in 1804, he married Miss Eliza Brown. Not, however, as a concession to society, but out of a generous regard for her own wishes. She was ill, she had taken to her bed, she was dying; Jumel, who had set out on a journey, was overtaken and brought home; on her deathbed—stated to be so by the doctor in attendance—she begged Jumel to marry her, she implored him to give her his name to take with her into the next world, as a talisman to shield her from the consequences of earthly indiscretion. Jumel complied at once, as soon as a minister could be summoned. In the very shadow of death they were married, in her bedchamber in the house on Whitehall Street, in front of the doctor, and Nodine, the butler, and her serving maids. It was all extremely touching.

It was infinitely less touching the next morning when the newly pronounced Madame Jumel arose from her bed in the best of health and as merry as a cricket, and went for a drive in her fine carriage. It had all been a hoax, she had not been at the point of death, she had not even been ill, and Nodine and the doctor had known it all along. A hoax, all of it, except the marriage which no man might now put asunder. There is something immensely comic, something prodigiously pathetic too, in the spectacle of Jumel, that middle-aged man of the world, that shrewd, farseeing, successful merchant, that honorable simpleton, twiddled—choused—gammoned—bamboozled by that little minx, that mere baggage, from Providence.

It was perfectly obvious what she was after, aside

from the actual placing of her relations with Jumel on a permanent basis which he had possibly not envisaged—this marriage was to be her passport into that foreign land of New York society the borders of which, all legends to the contrary, had been so rigorously closed to her. Jumel, for his part, took it extremely well, and behaved like a sensible middle-aged gentleman who has been twiddled by a little minx from Providence. He stood by his bargain, and on April 9, 1804, in the midst of that savage campaign conducted by Colonel Burr for the Governorship of New York State, they were married once more, at St. Patrick's Cathedral, on Prince Street. Then they settled down to wait for that recognition which the world could surely no longer refuse them.

They had waited for four years before—they now waited for another six, and still hardly a friendly visiting footstep crossed their threshold, no gesture of greeting did honor to the occupant of the fine carriage, no neighborly mansion opened its doors in welcome to her. Jumel had his counting room—the town had not stopped buying his "choice fluids"— he had his Tontine Coffee House, he might come and go through the streets and be received with polite toleration, but for his lady there was no melting of society's icy disregard.

Through the open windows there must often, in the springtime, have come to them the sound of music and singing from some nearby residence; a gentleman playing the fashionable German flute, a lady strumming on the four-stringed guitar—for the violin was considered ungenteel—or the soprano

strains of *Queen Mary's Lament* following the more
male refrain of *Hark away to the Downs;* they must
frequently have heard the laughter and chatter of
those intimate little soirées, just a few friends in the
early evening, scattered about the drawing room on
the second floor to applaud each other's ballads and
obligatos and consume tea and rusks, or perhaps
some cake and a glass of wine. But they were not
invited; Jumel himself, perhaps, but he would not
have gone without her. *They* were never invited.
And their own home remained dark and silent,
mocking them with its great empty drawing room,
with its silver, and china, and rich furniture which
were never used, with its staff of servants who had
nothing to do. Just a light in the back room down-
stairs where he sat reading a book, it may be, listening to the monotonous prattle of the lady who was
now his wife.

Because, except for the fact that she had been to
France and that he had come from there, they can
never have had the slightest thing in common. He
was an educated, cultured gentleman of the world;
she was, through no fault of her own, a vulgar, ignorant, mannerless nonentity. One wonders how often
he cursed the beauty which had ensnared him, in the
presence of the raffish ostentation with which she
bedizened it and which she mistook for stylish refinement; how often, frankly, he longed to choke her
when she babbled giddily, and none too grammati-
cally, of utterly platitudinous matters; how often
he wished that he might have perished in Santo
Domingo when he contemplated the cheerless vista

of an endless succession of years to be spent in the company of this woman of no discrimination, whose one consuming ambition was to see herself enthroned in a society which had forgotten her existence; who sat in her window, reveling in the finery which she had not the intelligence to appreciate, and yearned for the moon to be placed in her shapely but fatally incompetent hands.

They had no children, they had no relations to turn to—his were all in France; she was, so she assured him, alone in the world—they had no basis for any intellectual companionship. They had only a house, and a carriage, and her pretty little French ways which he must have come to loathe; her little eccentric ways, too, which were to develop into such pathetic aberrations in a later day. One looks at those ten tragic years and one sees, surely, a pitifully lonely man, caught in the meshes of his own generous folly, superbly loyal to a stupendous delusion.

It could not last, not that way, on Whitehall Street. Whether she twiddled him again into doing it, talked and wheedled him into it, or whether he did it of his own accord is not clear. But he had made a fortune and could well afford to retire from business; what his marriage had not accomplished, a spectacular display of wealth might bring about. In 1810, therefore, he purchased the estate which had at one time been the property of Colonel Roger Morris, and more lately Marriner's Tavern, restored the house to its former splendor as one of the greatest mansions in the vicinity of New York, and gave it outright to his wife. Betsy Bowen of Providence was become Lady of that Manor in which Miss Mary Philipse of Yonkers had once reigned long before. Let New York society, that inner circle of old manorial families, open its eyes, and more especially its doors, and do homage to so great a lady. What a carriage had made impossible, perhaps the manor would render inevitable. . . .

10

It was a fine estate, running from river to river, on the road leading to Kingsbridge, in the township of Haarlem. Originally the farm property of Jacob Dyckman and of his wife Jannetje, it had been purchased in 1765, by Mr. Roger Morris, a member of the Royal Council, as the site for the mansion which he began at once to build on the mount for his wife, Miss Mary Philipse, that was, of Yonkers. A splendid site, from which—or rather from the top of the house which soon crowned it—one saw the Hudson and East Rivers, the Haarlem with Hell Gate, the Sound, the City of New York in the distance, a great stretch of country in Long Island and West Chester, and the hills of Staten Island.

And it was a splendid mansion which Mr. Morris built there for his lady. A two-storied mansion facing the south, with a gallery under its columned portico, and outer walls two feet thick lined with English brick. Built to stand a long, long time— for more than one hundred and fifty years already. In the basement, a fine wainscoted kitchen, twenty feet by thirty, with a fireplace nine feet wide, and the buttery, dairy, laundry and offices; reception rooms

WALL STREET AND THE BOWLING GREEN

New York City

and wide halls on the ground floor, and the lofty octagonal room at the rear, thirty-two feet by twenty-two, embellished by a handsome marble mantelpiece. A plain mahogany staircase leading to the upstairs bedrooms. Above, a plastered garret. Nineteen rooms in all, including the halls. A solid, spacious house, with extremely beautiful doorways, otherwise quite unadorned; a country house, built for durability and comfort, unconcerned with mere superficialities of decoration. A house built with infinite discrimination and care, for a great lady.

For some ten years she lived in it, and then there was trouble in the Colonies. Mr. Morris, who was a Loyalist, thought it best to retire to England until the storm blew over. This he did, in 1775—leaving Mrs. Morris to preside over the mansion—but the storm did not blow over, and in 1777 he returned to New York to be made a colonel in the British military establishment. But he did not return to his mansion on Mount Morris, for it had become, in the fall of 1776, the headquarters of a certain General George Washington. For about three months the octagonal room was used for courts martial, as a result of which it received its subsequent name of "court martial room," while the General worked in his little office on the second floor; and then, in November, 1776, the house changed hands, becoming the headquarters of the British General, Lord Clinton, and after him of the Hessian commander, Lieutenant General Baron von Knyphausen, a name which must have rung strangely in those spacious halls.

As the property of a Loyalist the estate had, of

course, been confiscated, and after the peace it was
sold by the Commissioners of Forfeiture to Mr. John
Berrian and Mr. Isaac Ledyard. For several years
it passed from hand to hand, not excepting that of
Mr. John Jacob Astor who, in 1809, bought up all
the claims of the contesting heirs to the Morris and
Philipse manors, with the legal right to transfer for
which, in 1828, New York State seems to have paid
him half a million dollars. When, in 1810, the house
came into the possession of Jumel, it had in turn
served as farm building, road house and tavern,
under various names—Calumet Hall, Marriner's—
and under many proprietors.

Jumel was a man of excellent taste, and of more
than adequate wealth for the task of restoration
which he now undertook. Samples of the famous
wall paper in the court martial room—the green
panels with a border of doves, morning glories and
urns mounted on buckram—were sent to Paris for
duplication; every variety of equipment and furnish-
ing in keeping with the original character of the
house was provided; every detail of its former appearance was meticulously reproduced. Once again,
with infinite discrimination and care, the mansion
was garnished and made ready for another equally,
though somewhat singularly, great lady.

They moved in. Additional farms were acquired,
the estate was enlarged, consolidated. One imagines
Jumel perhaps happier at this period than he had
been for many years. There were novelties to be
seen to, a whole new order of routine to claim his
daily attention, pride in the fields, and meadows, and

orchards spreading around the beautiful mansion which bore his name. There was also a little girl running along the stone-flagged walks, and chattering up and down the house; a little nine year old girl to bear his name—Mary Eliza Jumel—the orphan daughter of Polly Clarke, a half-sister of Madame Jumel, produced from somewhere by her aunt with no one knows what explanations and precautions, and adopted by her fine uncle, "the Frenchman" whom they spoke of sometimes at Providence, when they thought of Betsy Bowen.

There was only one thing lacking—the dust of approaching carriages on the Kingsbridge Road, a jingling of coach harness at the gates of the estate, some Whitehall Street family names for Nodine to announce at the door of the octagonal drawing room. It could only be a question of time now before they came. The Jumels waited for five years, five renewed years of embittered disappointment, and no carriages came. New York society had opened its eyes, perhaps, but not its heart, and certainly not its doors. . . .

II

Fifteen years had passed since Jumel had taken Miss Eliza Brown to live on Whitehall Street; fifteen years of neglect and social disdain, at the end of which he experienced the final mortification resulting from his discovery—in what manner is not clear— of the existence of a certain Mr. George Washington Bowen at Providence. For the first time in all those years of subjection to his wife's caprices—her death-

bed comedies and her stubborn assaults upon the
ramparts of society—Jumel seems to have lost his
temper. One pictures him rather pink in the face,
pop-eyed and stuttering, shocked to his aristocratic
fingertips, gesticulating fluently, and none too courteously, in front of that—that little nothing from
Providence. She, for her part, is reported to have
burst into a rage spiced with undecorous invective,
and to have threatened to shoot him with a pistol—
just for what reason is not so manifest, except that
there is nothing so fundamentally exasperating as the
spectacle of a dupe, especially when he ceases to be one.

There was an unpleasant scene, but they patched
it up between them. It was not in her plans, certainly, to break with her generous, her "dear Stephen," as she continued to call him. In his mind,
there may have been a necessity for keeping up
appearances, an obstinate refusal to provide society
with any further mockery at his expense; perhaps
in his big, kindly heart he was sorry for her; perhaps,
indeed, he was still fond of her. Perhaps, on the
other hand, she knew something. There is a hint,
in some later correspondence, of a transaction of
which she helped dispose of the proof. But New
York was no longer possible. The forlorn hope of
the manor had failed, they must try something else.
In 1815, in his barque *Eliza*, Jumel took his wife and
niece to France.

It turned out to be a brilliantly successful move.
After a sojourn at Bordeaux, for the purpose of
visiting Jumel's family and presenting his wife to
them—a domestic ceremony which still, after all

the years, suggests to the imagination certain elements of pathetic humor—the Jumels arrived at Paris just as the Emperor, fallen at Waterloo, was about to be handed over a prisoner to the English. Whether or not Jumel offered him a ship to convey him to America, whether or not Napoleon gave his traveling carriage to Jumel and the key to his army chest to Madame, the fact remains that they became a part of the Napoleonic legend and were welcomed with extended palms, at least, by the considerably impoverished Napoleonic nobility.

He was an immensely wealthy merchant from America, a *milliardaire*, no doubt, who offered ships and country estates to emperors; she was beautiful, vivacious, dazzling, full of charming little foreign ways; so gay, so piquant, with her little American oddities of behavior and her hesitating French— which covered such a multitude of unsuspected deficiencies. They took a private hotel on the rue de Rivoli, and Madame Jumel took the air in a private carriage in which the ladies of Paris, unlike those of New York, deemed it a privilege to be seen. Mary Eliza Jumel was sent to a fashionable boarding school. The whole social world of the French capital paid its court to the lady from Haarlem; doors were opened everywhere; the butler had many great names to announce. Betsy Bowen was become the intimate friend of duchesses. They must have been very happy for a while; it was rain after prolonged drought, the cool shade of trees after burning deserts, the laughter and companionship of fellow-beings after long isolation. At all events, it was a triumph.

And then, suddenly, in December, 1816, something happened.   Perhaps the air of Paris went to Betsy's head; perhaps, already, she was spending too much money; perhaps Jumel grew tired of the masquerade and reminded her of Providence.   In any case, Madame Jumel found it necessary to return to America, alone, "because of her health."   Jumel went on a voyage to Italy; Madame, and Mary Eliza who joined her in 1817, remained at the mansion at Haarlem until 1821.   Four terrible, empty years for Betsy—except for the child and a surreptitious looking up of estranged half-brothers and sisters— for at the time she had not yet begun to people the spacious halls with the imaginary visitors of her demented later years.

But they patched it up again.   There seems to have been no end to Jumel's forbearance or, possibly, to his infatuation.   In 1821, Madame Jumel returned to Paris with her niece.   For five years they all lived in great state on the Place Vendome; they traveled, they entertained, they spent an enormous amount of money; Madame Jumel attended the Court; Madame Jumel's carriage—carriages seem to have played an important part in her life—her carriage was "noticed" by His Majesty, Louis XVIII.   It was a second triumph.

It was also an extremely expensive one.   The immensely wealthy merchant from America was beginning to see the bottom lining whenever he looked into his money bags; partly as a result of the lavish style which he had been maintaining, partly in consequence of an unending lawsuit which he had under-

taken in the hope of recovering from the French
Government the value of two ships and cargoes
seized by the officials of the port of Bayonne during
Napoleonic days. Perhaps he quarreled with his
wife over her extravagances; perhaps she sensed
the impending collapse of his fortune; perhaps the
burden of incompatibility which they had been
carrying was become too heavy.

This time a permanent separation, though friendly,
would seem to have been intended. Jumel was still
generous and munificent. In January, 1825, he
confirmed his gift to his wife of the mansion and the
lands which had formed the estate at the time of its
purchase. In addition, he deeded to her for life his
property on the corner of Broadway and Liberty
Street. Then, because he was in pressing need of
funds, and because he trusted this woman for whom
he had done so much, he gave her his power of attorney. Madame Jumel returned to America with
Mary Eliza, in 1826, armed with her husband's
signed authority—

" . . . for him, and in his name, and for his use,
and in his behalf to sell, either by public auction or
private contract as she shall think fit and see best;
for the price or prices that can be had or gotten, and
for his most benefit and advantage, all or any part
of the real estate that he may have belonging to him
and lying in the State of New York. . . ."

12

There is so little left to tell.

For two years, Jumel remained in France, selling

his household silver piece by piece to meet his rent, and imploring Madame Jumel to complete her negotiations in his behalf and send him the money which must be accumulating to his account. For two years Madame Jumel exercised her husband's power of attorney; and at the end of that time all of his property was safely in the hands of Miss Mary Eliza Jumel, and he was an utterly ruined man. Even the mansion itself now stood on the records in Mary's name. Jumel had been twiddled again, twiddled out of his lands and the money which was to have assured the comfort of his few remaining years, as once before he had been twiddled out of his name. For sheer simplicity of cold-blooded treachery the transaction has few equals.

The closing scenes are infinitely pathetic. It was not enough that he should have wasted thirty years of his life with her and have been swindled by her at the end; it was written that he must come begging her grudging charity, content to sit obscurely for a little while in a corner of the mansion, which had been his generous gift to her in the days of his prosperity. He arrived at New York in 1828, a discouraged old man in his seventies, still not quite credulous of what they had done to him, a querulous old man who was in the way. They let him stay at the mansion; all alone the first winter, then as a poor dependent who must be tolerated, and given his scraps, and his bit of fire. All alone in a corner with his thoughts and his memories, his broken heart and his impotent little reproaches.

He died on May 22, 1832, from injuries sustained

in a fall from a haycart.   He was buried in the cheer-
less enclosure of the churchyard of St. Patrick's
Cathedral, on Prince Street, under a plain stone.
A pitiful old gaffer—Stephen Jumel, merchant.

Madame Jumel was then fifty-seven years old.
She was still to become Madame Burr, and to live
to be ninety.   A fantastic old woman, all alone with
her memories and her hallucinations, her disordered
mind, and her banquets spread for imaginary guests.
She died on July 16, 1865, all powdered and rouged,
and covered with jewels, and was buried in a great
tomb, far away from Prince Street.   A pitiful old
gammer—Betsy Bowen, adventuress. . . .

II
William Eaton, Hero

WILLIAM EATON, HERO

I

IN the closing years of the eighteenth century, three merry monarchs sat on embroidered divans in their respective palaces and viewed the maritime commerce of the Mediterranean Sea with a glittering eye. They were the Dey of Algiers, the Bey of Tunis and the Bashaw of Tripoli, three fat, bearded, rapacious ruffians clinking with jewels, whose xebecs, polacres, galliots and galleasses went darting in and out of their inhospitable harbors on a dangerous, windswept coast, swooping down on hapless merchantmen, and dragging their Christian crews away to slavery and the whiplashed rowers' benches.

For three centuries these corsairs of the high coast of Barbary had been indulging in this remunerative pastime; harrying the shores of their inland sea, pushing out into the Atlantic, and as far as Iceland, bringing swift terror and destruction into harbors of the British Isles, and chivying the dignified Dutch up the Channel with bloodthirsty outcries. Ever since the days of Horuk and Khair-ed-Din at Tunis, in 1500, and of Hasan Aga at Algiers; so that Spain, and Genoa, and Venice were frequently obliged to contrive tremendous armadas against the Infidels, with varying results. In 1530, for instance, when Charles V conquered Tunis and massacred thirty thousand men, women and children like a good Christian; and in 1541, when, with an army led by Captain Hernando Cortes and a great fleet commanded by Andrea Doria, the Genoese, he tried his luck against Algiers in the presence of many great ladies of Spain come to witness the emperor's victory —only to lose most of the ladies and one hundred and fifty vessels in a hurricane, and see his army cut to pieces ashore in, perhaps, one of history's most lurid disasters; and again, as late as 1775, when renewed disaster at the hands of that same Algiers overtook another Spanish expedition of four hundred ships.

And now in the late 1790's, "seven kings of Europe and two republics" were purchasing annual security from these worthies, and Consuls of Great Britain, of Denmark, of Spain, were pocketing their pride and offering an enormous yearly tribute, in return for permission to use the Mediterranean from three little African nabobs whom it was easier to placate than to punish—although the hope that some of the nations concerned might fall from financial grace and so lose their commerce was not absent from the minds of the tributary governments, not a few of which considered Algiers an excellent handicap to the prosperity of their rivals.

And from this group of hand kissing, palm greasing Consuls, those of the young American republic were not absent. For America was carrying on a profitable trade in the Mediterranean with very few ships

of war to protect it, and while her envoys at Paris
might shout "Millions for defense, not one cent for
tribute!" in Citizen Talleyrand's ear, at Algiers, and
everywhere in Barbary, her consular agents paid
their dues and did their shouting at home. Thirty
thousand dollars to Morocco in 1795; one million
dollars to Algiers in 1793, and another million in
1797, to say nothing of an annual contribution of
twenty-two thousand dollars in naval stores; one
hundred thousand dollars to Tunis; eighty-three
thousand dollars to Tripoli; and the Treasury only
knew what other sums in jewels, and "consular
presents," and "usances." Such was the mortifying
situation when Captain William Eaton was sent as
United States Consul to Tunis, in 1798.

2

He was a young man in his thirties, nearly six feet
tall, with a fair, ruddy complexion and large blue
eyes, and of commanding aspect. A quick tempered, fiery young man with a chip on his shoulder;
bold, fearless, independent, voluble and indiscreet;
a young man of intellect, resource and eloquence.
A Connecticut Yankee, born at Woodstock, on February 23, 1764, the second child among thirteen of
schoolmaster-farmer Nathan Eaton and his wife
Sarah.

As a boy, already, William was rash and adventurous, always falling off the top of the barn and out
of apple trees, so that he came near breaking his neck
on countless occasions; but in the fields at Mansfield,
to which the family had moved when he was ten,

William was always shirking his work to sit in the shade and read some book purloined from his father's shelves—for his was a nature curiously compounded of studious instincts, so that at one time he thought of becoming a minister, and of energetic impulses which finally turned him into a soldier. He was only sixteen when he ran away from home to join the Continental troops, and when they sent him back ill, he returned to the army as soon as he was able and became a sergeant at seventeen. There followed years of Latin and Greek, during which "his mind was most seriously affected with religious impressions," and in 1787—after an earlier failure due to his inability to keep up with his classes while absent all winter long at his schoolmastering—he walked from Mansfield to Hanover, in New Hampshire, with "one pistareen of money" in his pocket and some pins and needles to sell on the way, and matriculated as a Freshman at Dartmouth College. During the winters he still taught school, as was permissible for impecunious students, but he found time to act in a college dramatic performance and to write some magnificently bad verse, and in August, 1790, he received his Bachelor's degree.

For a while he served as Clerk to the House of Delegates of Vermont, and in March, 1792, secured a captaincy. In August of that year he married a widow of twenty-five summers, Mrs. Eliza Danielson, who was destined to see very little of him for a good many years to come, and in the fall he was ordered to the Army of the West, on the Ohio. A brief leave of absence in 1794 and they set him to

GENERAL WILLIAM EATON

recruiting for a year, and in December, 1795, he
sailed with his company from Philadelphia, to the
Army of the South this time, in Georgia. A tempestuous journey which he described to his wife in a
metrical explosion in which much, perhaps, of this
extravagant, madcap poet, scholar, soldier, orator,
paladin is revealed—

"Hoarse through the cordage growled the threatening blast,
  Portentous of the storm. The expanse of Heaven
  O'ercast with murky columns, seemed convulsed
  With one wide waste of elemental war.
  From every point along the bounding surges
  Rolled the black phalanx of electric fluid.
  Borne on the pinions of the maddening storm . . .
  Down rushed the glaring tempest, rain and hail,
  In winding torrents closed, and the vast space
  Of sea and air seemed one promiscuous deluge.
  Blue streams of angling sulphur blazed around
  Transforming midnight to the fire of day,
  Reserving all her horrors. Peals on peals
  Burst from the flaming batteries of Heaven
  And naught but horror stalked along the gloom . . ."

In other words, there was quite a thunder storm off
Hatteras.

They kept him in Georgia, imprudently arguing
with his Colonel Commandant, until 1796, and
then he was courtmartialed, for speculating in army
supplies, for disobedience, for anything which the
Colonel Commandant could think of. But the War
Department did not confirm the verdict of suspension
passed by a court which, in the opinion of one of its
own members, was very partial to "our Colonel
Commandant who is an ignorant, debauched, un-

principled old bachelor," willing to "sacrifice the
purest character to gratify the spleen of his soul."
Captain Eaton was ordered to Philadelphia, entrusted with various confidential missions for the
State Department, and, in July, 1797, appointed to
his consular post at Tunis.   He sailed, on December
22, 1798, aboard the United States brig *Sophia*,
accompanied by four other vessels to be delivered to
the Dey of Algiers for "arrearages of present dues."

3

Eaton carried with him a Letter of Credence from
President John Adams to the Bey of Tunis, "the well
guarded City and Abode of Felicity," Hamouda
Pasha,

"the most illustrious and most magnificent Prince,
who commands the Odgiac of Tunis, the abode of
happiness; and the most honored Ibrahim Dey, and
Soliman, Aga of the Janisaries and Chief of the Divan,
and all the elders of the Odgiac."

Aside from that, he was to coöperate with the Consuls at Algiers and at Tripoli in rectifying certain
unsatisfactory clauses in a treaty recently made
with Tunis.
    Eaton found the most illustrious and most magni-
ficent Prince to be a "huge, shaggy beast sitting on
his rump," as he elegantly expressed it, who permitted the new Consul to kiss his hand, and listened
dubiously to his observations concerning the treaty.
Whereupon there arose into the azure sky of felicitous

Tunis a general litany of insinuating suggestions from every official in the palace—for jewels, for swords, for rich cloths, for gunpowder, for stores, for whole ships, and for money—which endured for months and nearly drove Eaton crazy. Ever a reluctant renderer even unto Cæsar of the things that were Cæsar's, Eaton boiled with rage and was consumed with patriotic mortification at the spectacle of this gaudy bandit who sat crosslegged on a sofa and prefaced every slight concession which he deigned to consider with a demand for more tribute. But he persevered in his task, and finally, in April, 1800, the desired alterations to the treaty were accomplished, as a result of the timely arrival of the *Hero* with long overdue "presents" and stores.

But this was only a pause in the chorus of Tunisian mendicancy, and for three years Eaton was to hear nothing but insults and abuse in one ear, and peremptory, threatening demands in the other, culminating in the Bey's request for a thirty-six gun frigate with which, no doubt, to offend the eyes of his fellow monarchs at Algiers and Tripoli. And when Eaton advised him to whistle for his frigate, the "Prince of the Princes of Tunis" wrote a letter himself to "Sir President," in 1802, in reply to which Mr. Jefferson informed his "great and good friend, the most illustrious and most magnificent Prince, the Bey of Tunis," that he had no frigates to spare. One is inclined to laugh at all this tomfoolery until one reads Eaton's letter of almost the same date to Secretary of State Madison, in which that courageous Yankee was obliged to confess to his chief that—

"My exile is become insupportable here. . . .
No advice from Government to regulate my conduct,
and my own exertions failing of effect; I am left subject, though not yet submissive, to the most intoler-
able abuse and personal vexation. Anxiety, per-
plexity, and a climate unfavorable to my constitution waste my health."

And in the meantime, things had not been going
so well at Algiers, and one imagines poor Eaton fairly
bursting with fury at the news which reached him
from that port. For in September, 1800, Captain
Bainbridge, in the twenty-four gun frigate *George
Washington*, had presented himself before the mole
at Algiers for the purpose of paying the annual
Algerine tribute. A duty none too congenial to the
commander of an American war ship, but there was
further disgrace unspeakable to be experienced. Algiers was in trouble at Constantinople, there was an
embassy to be sent to the Grand Signior Sultan and
presents to soothe his anger. Mustapha, Dey of
Algiers, gazed upon the American frigate anchored
under the guns of his powerful shore batteries and
had a luminous inspiration. The American frigate
would take his Ambassador to Constantinople.

"You pay me tribute," he reminded the protesting
Bainbridge, "by which you become my slaves. I
have, therefore, a right to order you as I may think
proper."

And not only that, but the frigate would fly the
Algerine flag at the main. Bainbridge, at the mercy
of the Dey's batteries, had no choice in the matter of
the errand to Constantinople, but to haul down the

American flag, thereby putting his frigate out of commission, was something to break his sailor's heart. He would fly the Algerine flag at the fore, out of courtesy to the Ambassador, and that was all. No, the Dey assured him, he would fly it at the main —and his General of Marine came aboard with a troop of soldiers, climbed up to the maintop, tore down the American flag and put the Algerine standard in its place. Bainbridge looked at the maintop, then he looked at the guns covering his ship and realized that the destruction of the frigate would do more harm to American commerce than that piece of bunting flying at his masthead. He swallowed very hard, therefore, and sat back to watch the embarkation of an extraordinary ship's company. The Ambassador and his suite of one hundred, bringing with them nearly one million dollars' worth of presents and cash; one hundred negro women and their children; one hundred and fifty sheep, twenty-five heads of cattle and four horses; and twelve parrots, four antelopes, four lions and four tigers.

And so, on October 19, this floating menagerie which had once been an American frigate set sail for Constantinople, a sort of Turkish Noah's Ark from whose decks arose the clamorous bedlam of a variety of incongruous beasts. The very moment she was out of range of the batteries the Algerine flag came down, and all the Americans aboard felt better, so that good humor intervened, in a measure, to relieve the mortification of their employment. For three weeks they went screeching and bellowing on their way, tacking back and forth to the unending con-

fusion of the Faithful striving to keep their prayerful
countenances turned to the East—and then they
were at Constantinople, the first American ship to
enter that harbor. The Turks were delighted and
interested—what was that flag, what were the
United States? A new world discovered some time
before, it seemed, by Christopher Columbus. Well,
well, Allah was indeed great. Bainbridge was fêted
by the authorities, he formed a lasting friendship
with the Turkish Admiral who gave him a salute
from Tapana Fortress never before accorded to a
foreign vessel, and in December the *George Washington* returned to Algiers, with a message from the
Sultan to the Dey which caused the latter to blink
in considerable trepidation. And this time the
frigate anchored beyond the range of the Algerine
guns. . . .

And at Tripoli things were not going at all. For
some time the Bashaw, Yusuf the bloody, of the
House of the Karamanli, had been turning over in
his avaricious mind the fact that he was not receiving
as much tribute from America as his "cousins" of
Algiers and Tunis. In April, 1801, he demanded a
payment of two hundred and twenty-five thousand
Spanish dollars and an annual contribution of twenty-
five thousand more, and when his ultimatum was
rejected he declared war on the United States, on
May 10, in the traditional Tripolitan manner, by
cutting down the flagstaff of the American consulate.

During that summer the war was carried on by
four ships under Commodore Dale, who did what he
could, blockading the coast and capturing enemy

WILLIAM EATON, HERO 63

grain ships, until his return to America, in December. He was followed by Commodore Morris, a courageous officer somewhat lacking in initiative, who backed and filled rather aimlessly up and down the Mediterranean until his recall in the spring of 1803; so that Eaton advised Mr. Madison that Government might as well "send out Quaker meeting houses to float about this sea, as frigates with Murrays in command." In fact, it seemed to him in 1802 that "the operations of our squadron this season have done less than the last to aid my efforts," and in December of that year "only one frigate of this squadron has been hitherto seen on the enemy's coast." The war was dragging along, into the summer of 1803, and nothing was being accomplished except to convince Yusuf Bashaw that the Americans were very small pumpkins indeed, when Commodore Preble was sent out to relieve the floundering Morris.

4

From the very beginning of his sojourn at Tunis, and increasingly so with the advent of the Tripoli war, Eaton had squirmed under his government's pusillanimous policy, and had advocated forceful measures to silence the insulting demands of the Barbary brotherhood once and for all. If America was going to spend money in Africa let her spend it on ships of war, and if gunpowder was to be contributed to the corsairs let it be used to fire American guns at their strongholds. A powerful squadron, a little determination and above all a little national pride would do the trick. To his impetuous, energetic, uncompromising Yankee way of thinking there had been too much of this unnecessary humiliation, this loaning of frigates, this constant purchasing of shameful favors, this timid backbending before three insignificant little princelings.

And so he turned his thoughts into any channel which might lead to a more prompt consummation of the vengeance upon the Bashaw of Tripoli, and looked under every pebble in his path in the hope of discovering some means of further damage to that brigand. And under one of these pebbles he found Sidi Mahomet, the son of Karaman, who was commonly called Hamet. Now this Karaman had been Bashaw of Tripoli some nine years before, and at his death he had left three sons, Hasan, Hamet and Yusuf. To Hasan, and after him to Hamet, should have gone the embroidered sofa of Tripoli, but Yusuf had caused him to be slaughtered—a fate which Hamet escaped only by precipitate flight—and seized the sofa for his own. And now, in 1801, Yusuf the usurper was Bashaw of Tripoli, and Hamet was living precariously at Tunis itself, enjoying the protection and charity of the Bey who doubtless saw in him an instrument of possible annoyance to his colleague of Tripoli, should occasion ever arise. Which was precisely what Eaton saw in him, and the occasion arisen.

Eaton looked at Hamet Karamanli for a while with a speculative interest, and then a splendidly adventurous, though by no means impractical, vision began to take shape in his imagination. With the American squadron attacking Tripoli from the

THE BURNING OF THE U. S. FRIGATE "PHILADELPHIA" IN THE HARBOR OF TRIPOLI

sea—if these precious sailors could ever be induced
to do anything except tramp up and down their
quarterdecks and cock their eye at the wind—he
would take Hamet out of his Tunisian seclusion,
bolster him up with American supplies and marines
and lead him across the sands in a land assault on
Tripoli which would take the usurper in the rear
and place the rightful Bashaw on his throne. One
imagines Eaton stalking into Hamet's chamber one
day, six feet of blue-eyed Yankee aflame with an
idea, and overwhelming the Pretender with a flow
of passionate oratory, poking him in the back, and
generally disturbing the tobacco-scented peace of
that rather mildly disposed and very slightly heroic
individual.

"Now see here, Hamet, I'm your friend, and I'm
going to put you back on your throne if you'll say
the word. . . ."

It must all have seemed extremely improbable to
Hamet, and most astonishing, and not particularly
alluring, perhaps. But Eaton talked to him, and
pestered him, and probably bullied him, until of
two evils—the enmity of his murderous brother and
the eloquence of this implacable American—the
bewildered Hamet chose the lesser, and decided to
attack Yusuf. At all events, in September, 1801,
Eaton was already writing to Mr. Madison concerning—

"a project in concert between the rightful Bashaw
of Tripoli, now an exile in Tunis, and myself, to
attack the usurper by land while our operations are
going on by sea. . . . The Bey of Tunis, though

prudence will keep him behind the curtain, I have strong reasons to believe will cheerfully promote the scheme."

But wherever the Bey may have kept himself, there seem to have been other persons behind the curtain for it was not long before Yusuf at Tripoli was aware of these machinations, and in December he sent overtures of friendship to his brother Hamet and offered him the Governorship of Derne. Eaton, absent at the time on a voyage to Leghorn for his health, returned in the early spring of 1802 to find a subdued and mollified Hamet who wanted nothing from his friend except a passport to Tripoli to go and see his family and make his peace with his brother. But Eaton did not propose to lose his Pretender so easily; he refused the passport, and—

"told him candidly that if he departed we must consider him in the light of an enemy, and that instead of my influence to assist his passage to Tripoli I should give it to have him and his retinue carried prisoner of war to the United States; but if he would adhere to his former arrangements I did not doubt but that before the expiration of four months he might be offered to his people by an American squadron. I tell him the sole object of his brother is to cut his throat. He is sufficiently alarmed and much distressed. . . ."

Eaton was more or less talking through his white consular hat; especially as the captains of the squadron, Bainbridge, and Murray, and the others, were definitely opposed to the whole scheme of a land expedition—if for no other reason, because they were all hostile to this obstreperous Consul, this former army officer turned civilian, who presumed to criticize the conduct of the naval forces and kept harping on that episode of the Algerine flag aboard the *George Washington*. But Hamet was frankly terrified, and now he was in even worse straits, for the Bey of Tunis had suddenly cut off his supplies, no doubt in answer to a hint from the Bashaw, a hint adorned, it may be, with jewels. Hamet proposed to retire to Malta; Eaton insisted on his selecting Leghorn or Sardinia, and talked of armed ships to go after him if he went elsewhere. But Hamet finally had his way, for once, and in August he was at Malta, receiving money from Eaton "on the credit of the United States," and bloodcurdling accounts of Yusuf's intentions towards his person if he set foot in either Derne or Tripoli. At the same time he was maintaining a brisk correspondence with his adherents on the mainland, while brother Yusuf scratched his ear and began to wonder where all this might terminate.

And now Eaton himself was in a predicament. His negotiations and transactions with Hamet had involved an expense of twenty-three thousand dollars which he had borrowed, and which must now be repaid. And he was destitute of resources; if this expense "should not be admitted in account on final settlement, my property in America must go to indemnify the United States so far as it will extend to that object." That was in November, 1802. In December, "my means and my resources of resistance

are totally exhausted at this place. . . . I can no
longer talk of resistance and coercion without exciting
a grimace of contempt and ridicule." And in March,
1803, he was "totally destitute of funds and credit
here, and do not know where to obtain the means of
daily subsistence."

He was determined to return to America; a decision
which delighted the Bey, who found him "too obstinate and too violent for me. I must have a Consul
with a disposition more congenial to Barbary interests!" Commodore Morris came to Tunis to
take Eaton aboard, and was promptly arrested for
the Consul's debts. But the business was finally
adjusted, and, on March 10, Eaton departed from
the Abode of Felicity, or, depending on the point of
view, from "this sink of treachery."

5

The State Department having refused to accept
Eaton's Hamet accounts, he spent the summer of
1803 at Brimfield, Massachusetts, with the family
which he had not seen for nearly five years, and
returned to Washington in January, 1804, for the
session of Congress which was to investigate his
claims. But he had not forgotten Hamet, or his
scheme for an expedition to Tripoli, and he lost no
opportunity to interest the government in his venture—which, he maintained, would have been successful in 1802 if he had been properly seconded
by a commander "who employed the whole oper-
ative naval force of the United States an entire
year in the Mediterranean attending the travels

of a woman!" No wonder he was hated by the Navy.

But there was a new commander in the Mediterranean now, the energetic Commodore Preble. And although the unlucky Bainbridge and three hundred Americans had been captured by the Tripolitans, and dragged half naked before the delighted Bashaw, at the time of the disaster to the *Philadelphia*, the whole country was ringing, in the spring of 1804, with Lieutenant Stephen Decatur's exploit of sailing into the harbor of Tripoli and setting fire to the captured frigate, so that she blew up with terrifying detonations under the Bashaw's windows, while the imprisoned Americans yelled their heads off and jeered at the flabbergasted Tripolitan cannoniers. And not only that, but Hamet himself had crossed over to Derne, placed himself at the head of an Arab army and inflicted important reverses on his brother's forces—a circumstance which shows him not to have been the utterly spineless creature which certain chronicles have tried to make of him, and which puts Eaton's project in a less fantastic light, with its revelation of the native support which Hamet, given adequate funds, was able to command.

Hamet was quite pleased with himself, and wrote to tell Mr. Jefferson about it and to ask him for help, and, in March, the President decided to send him some supplies, some artillery, a thousand stands of arms, and forty thousand dollars. He also appointed Eaton Navy Agent to the Barbary States for the purpose of assisting Hamet's campaign. This was going a long way for that gingerly administration, and when, along in May, news reached Washington that Hamet had been obliged to retire to Alexandria for lack of those very supplies, Mr. Jefferson changed his mind. The supplies were countermanded. "On the first symptoms of a reverse," Eaton wrote in a private letter,

"discouragement superseded resolution with our Executive, and economy supplanted good faith and honesty. . . . The Secretary of War believes we had better pay tribute. He said this to me in his own office. Gallatin . . . shrinks behind the counter. Mr. Madison leaves everything to the Secretary of the Navy."

And the Secretary of the Navy said to Commodore Barron, who was taking Eaton out with a new squadron—

"With respect to the ex-Bashaw of Tripoli we have no objection to your availing yourself of his cooperation with you against Tripoli, if you shall . . . consider his cooperations expedient. The subject is committed entirely to your discretion. In such an event you will, it is believed, find Mr. Eaton extremely useful to you."

At the same time, Commodore Barron was to make peace with Tripoli whenever, in his opinion, a suitable opportunity presented itself.

So that, when Eaton sailed, in June, 1804, aboard the *John Adams* in company with the frigates *President*, *Congress*, *Essex* and *Constellation*, without specific instructions and with no definite assurances

of executive support, he had no illusions concerning
the rôle to which he was destined.

"The cautious policy of the President," he wrote,
"is calculated to evade responsibility as well as to
secure to himself all the advantages of a miracle;
for . . . he neither sends forward supplies nor
even makes any reply to the chief of whose friendship he is willing to profit. If, therefore, the cooperation fail of success he evades the imputation
of having embarked in a speculative, theoretical,
chimerical project. This will fix on me. Whereas
if it succeeds the glory of the enterprise will be all
his own, ascribed to his foresight and sagacity . . .
I can say, as a Spartan Ambassador to the King of
Persia's lieutenant, when asked whether he came
with a public commission or on his own account—
If successful for the public, if unsuccessful for myself."

6

In September, 1804, Eaton was once more in that
turbulent Mediterranean, at Malta, and in December,
at Syracuse where Commodore Barron was taking
over the command from Preble. And the retiring
Commodore had much to relate concerning the activities of the previous months. In August, there had
been a tremendous attack on Tripoli, in which Lieutenant Decatur had gone careering up and down the
harbor with his gunboats providing the material for
countless patriotic prints, while the frigates treated the town to a bombardment which drove the
Bashaw into the nearest cellar. But Yusuf knew his
Barbary weather and refused to make peace, counting
on a convenient norther to scatter the American

squadron. Four times during the next month the
fleet repeated its demonstrations without success,
and the fifth time dreadful disaster overtook Captain
Somers and his crew of volunteers in the fire ship
Intrepid; she blew up into smithereens at the en-
trance to the harbor—Somers having, presumably,
touched her off with his own hand upon finding
himself boarded by the enemy—and here the squadron was back at Syracuse, and the Bashaw back on
his sofa, biting his thumb at Bainbridge and the
captive Americans. As for Hamet, he was supposed
to be at Alexandria, waiting for some word from
America.

On November 14, therefore, Eaton sailed for
Malta and Alexandria, aboard the brig *Argus*, Captain Isaac Hull in command, taking with him a
written memorandum signed by Hull of the verbal
instructions issued by Commodore Barron to Hull
in Eaton's presence. His official, written orders
were, it seems—

". . . intended to disguise the real object of
your expedition; which is to proceed with Mr. Eaton
to Alexandria in search of Hamet Bashaw . . .
and to convey him to Derne or such place . . .
most proper for cooperating with the naval forces
under my command against the common enemy.
. . . The Bashaw may be assured of the support
of my squadron at Bengazi or Derne . . . and
you may assure him also that I will take the most
effectual measures with the forces under my command for cooperating with him against the usurper,
his brother, and for reestablishing him in the regency
of Tripoli. Arrangements to this effect with him

are confided to the discretion with which Mr. Eaton is vested by the Government."

Instructions which may or may not have caused Eaton to smile, since he knew himself to be vested by Government with all the discretion in the world, provided that he abstain from any expectation of being upheld should such a course prove inconvenient to the administration. But as a matter of fact he took them quite seriously; he was to help put Hamet back on his throne of Tripoli, and Commodore Barron was to "take the most effectual measures" to bring this about; Eaton's dream was coming true, and the "expedition to Egypt" was under way. The blue-eyed Yankee must have been very happy, crossing his fondly anticipated bridges.

The *Argus* arrived at Alexandria on November 25. Hamet was not there; he was at Cairo, he was up the river, he had joined the Mamelukes—no one knew just where Hamet was. Eaton and the officers assigned to him went to Rosetta, took a river boat up the Nile and reached Cairo on December 8. After a triumphant entry on horseback—escorted by Turkish officers and followed everywhere by gaping crowds—they rode in state, preceded by a torchlight procession, through seething streets to the Viceroy's palace where they were received by guards of honor, and ushered into the audience hall in which, on a sofa of embroidered purple and damask, the Viceroy greeted them with coffee, tobacco and sherbets.

And after suitable conversational philanderings

they came at last to the subject of Hamet. Where
was Hamet? Well, Hamet, left practically destitute
at Alexandria, had joined the revolted Mamelukes
and was at that moment besieged with some of their
Beys in the village of Miniet in Upper Egypt. An
awkward circumstance, since, aside from the fact
of his being now a rebel against Turkish authority,
it was questionable whether the Mameluke Beys
would allow him to depart from their midst. But as
far as the Turks were concerned, the Viceroy was
very reasonable about it all; he granted Hamet a
letter of amnesty and permission to pass the Turkish
lines, and sent couriers to bring him to Cairo. And
in the meantime, Eaton had sent couriers of his own,
to inform him that—

"I am the American Consul who made an agree-
ment with your Excellency previously to your departure from Tunis for Malta. I have since been
home; my Government have approved of my conduct and I am now come out to fulfill my promises.
Let me know how I can communicate with your
Excellency without embroiling myself with the Grand
Signior whom I honor and respect. America is at
peace with all the world except your brother Joseph—
we will never make peace with him. I am your
Excellency's sincere friend."

Promises, assurances, prophecies—Eaton's utter-
ances were always the children of his hopes. . . .

7

And of all the strange characters who were to take
part in the forthcoming desert melodrama, there was

none more strange, perhaps, than the courier who reached Hamet with this letter—the astonishing "Eugene Leitensdorfer." Born in 1772, near Trent in the Tyrol, Gervasio Santuari abandoned the religious studies in which he was engaged, to marry, at an early age, a young woman who does not seem to have enjoyed any great share of his subsequent attention. After studying engineering and surveying, he entered the Austrian army, took part in the expedition against Belgrade, and found himself eventually at the siege of Mantua, from which he departed one night to join the French at Milan, under the name of Carlo Hossondo. Suspected by them, however, of being a spy, he poisoned his guards with opium and escaped to Switzerland, adopting for the purpose the name of Johan Eugene Leitensdorfer. With the money which his family contrived to send him, he then purchased a stock of jewelry and watches and traveled extensively through France and Spain, until arriving at Toulon one day he embarked on a vessel for Egypt. In Egypt, he served the French until the English came, and then the English with equal facility, ran a coffee house, managed a theater and married a Coptic wife.

Upon the departure of the English from Egypt, he abandoned his coffee house, theater, wife and child, and retired to Messina, where, from temporary lack of anything more profitable to do, he entered himself as a novice in a Capuchin monastery in which he passed as Padre Anselmo. One pauses for breath, and finds him on a ship bound for Smyrna, from whence he soon drifted to Constantinople. There, for three days and nights, he went **without** food **or** drink, and finally borrowed a pack of cards with which to secure a few pennies by performing tricks. A little later he enlisted in the Turkish army—all armies were alike to Gervasio Carlo Johan Eugene Anselmo—and joined a disastrous expedition against Egypt, from which he escaped to the Arabs in the desert, to return eventually to Constantinople.

And then this extraordinary man decided to become a Dervish. He renounced his faith, underwent certain ritualistic ceremonies necessary to his new status and religion, called himself Murat Aga, and departed with a caravan to Trebizond. At Trebizond, the Bashaw was suffering from an affliction to his eyes; Murat Aga being a Dervish was also supposed to be a doctor; he blew the contents, very possibly unknown to him, of a paper of powder in the Bashaw's eye, prophesied a prompt recovery, and departed again, as rapidly as possible, with a caravan to Persia. But messengers overtook him to announce the miraculous recovery of the Bashaw—a circumstance which Murat Aga had not altogether anticipated—so he returned to Trebizond to be loaded with gifts, enjoyed a season of honorable repose and betook himself to Mecca before some other less amenable ailment should befall the Bashaw. From Mecca he went to Jedda, on the Red Sea, crossed over to Suez, and, grown weary of so much holiness, became interpreter to Lord Gordon, an English traveler who took him to Nubia and Abyssinia.

Finally, after an absence of six years, he found himself again in Alexandria, and remembered that

he had once had a wife there.   He made search for
her, for the purpose of securing a legal separation, and
returned to Cairo where he had found employment
as a military engineer when Eaton saw him, and chose
this tall, lean, agile, swarthy, young man of thirty-
two—who spoke so many languages and who had
played so many rôles—to be his courier. . . .

8

Eaton was waiting at Cairo, anxiously and impatiently, so that Egypt held no charms for him.

"I can," he wrote, "see nothing on the celebrated
Nile which the Ohio, Mississippi, Altamaha, Savan-
nah and Chesapeake do not offer us; even her croco-
diles and her *cajal* would have nothing to boast side
and side by our alligators and catfish. . . .   Ruined
temples, pyramids and catacombs, monuments of
the superstition, pride and folly of their founders,
disgust my sight."

But at last, in January, a messenger arrived from
Hamet.   He was coming—it is a pity, perhaps, to
deny the legend which describes Eaton plunging into
the desert, chivying Hamet out of his hiding place,
and dragging him back into the enforced limelight
of history—Hamet was coming, to a friendly Arab's
house at Fayoum, and Eaton might see him there.
But Eaton had already told him to come to Rosetta,
and believing that he would do so, went there to
meet him.   No Hamet.   This prudent Prince was
evidently suspicious of the Turks.   So, on January
22, with two officers and twenty-three men from the

Argus, "indifferently mounted," Eaton set out from Alexandria to join Hamet at Fayoum. On January 23 they were all arrested as British spies in the Turkish lines. But the Turks were always ready to listen to a good story and to investigate its authenticity. The Pacha in command listened to Eaton, and sent for an Arab Sheik of his acquaintance who confirmed the fact of Hamet's presence at Fayoum, and added that twenty thousand Arabs were prepared to follow him against Tripoli—for a consideration. The Pacha was impressed, sent the Sheik after Hamet, and treated Eaton with every courtesy, even though he did surround him with fierce-looking sentinels.

On February 5, Hamet arrived, without the twenty thousand Arabs, at the Turkish camp—and they met once more, those friends, Hamet the fugitive and Eaton the Bashaw maker; the fair-haired, blue-eyed, daredevil man from the West, and the black-bearded, dark-skinned, diffident man of the East. He remains, unfortunately, shadowy and featureless, the native, but one sees a certain unpretentious dignity, a considerable spontaneous courage and the shy, questioning resolve of an essentially timid man, come, a little against his inclination, perhaps, but of his own accord, to lay his trusting simplicity in another's hands. They met, and important words were spoken.

Two days later they left for Alexandria to embark aboard the *Argus*, and were promptly placed under arrest by another Turkish contingent until a *firman* from the Viceroy released them. And now it seemed that Hamet was determined to march overland to

Derne, about four hundred miles across the Desert of Barca. He pitched his camp, consequently, at the Arab's Tower, a little way out of Alexandria, to recruit the five hundred odd followers whom their resources allowed them to equip, while Eaton went into the city to make his arrangements with Captain Hull to meet them at the Bay of Bomba, to collect supplies and to prevent their being stolen by the Turks in whose ears the French Consul was whispering not wholly disinterested suggestions.

And since a good many thousands of dollars were involved, he made a "convention" with Hamet, which deserves to be preserved in that archive devoted to America's unratified treaties. A convention whereby the United States were to be indemnified out of the proceeds of the annual tribute to Tripoli from Sweden, Denmark and Holland, and no ransom required for the three hundred Americans now held by Yusuf Bashaw. In return, the United States—in the person of William Eaton, "General and Commander in Chief of the Land Forces," who should have known better—pledged themselves to assist Hamet on land and sea to regain his throne. To regain his throne.

Once again, as expressed in the words which flowed so readily from Eaton's pen, the hope was father to the fact. Of course, there were those verbal instructions of Commodore Barron's! It may be that Eaton did not actually know that Barron was under orders to make peace with Tripoli at the first opportunity—or if he did, perhaps he did not believe that the Commodore would do so until the purpose of the

Derne expedition was accomplished. And of course the document was a nice souvenir, in any case, for Hamet. . . .

9

They assembled, on March 3, at the Arab's Tower. One hundred and seven camels and other beasts of burden with their drivers; a troop of Arab horsemen led by two Sheiks; the ninety men of Hamet's personal escort; thirty-eight Greeks with two officers; twenty-five miscellaneous cannoniers with three officers; six American marines from the *Argus* under the command of a sergeant, a midshipman, Mr. Peck, and Lieutenant O'Bannon; a doctor picked up at Alexandria—an Englishman called Farquhar—the inevitable Leitensdorfer—Hamet Bashaw and "General" Eaton. Perhaps four hundred persons of all colors and creeds, wild men from the desert in flowing white, scrapings of Alexandria in heterogeneous raiment, a parcel of Greeks descended, it may be, from the Ten Thousand of that other March to the Sea, a handful of unexcited Americans with one eye on the Greeks and the other on the provision camels, the Sheiks, Generals and Excellencies—and Midshipman Peck, very dignified, no doubt, in his brass buttoned blue coat and red waistcoat, his high standing collar and black stock, and the little dirk hanging from a chain at his left hip. Very dignified, and enormously interested, and excessively hot. They marched, at eleven o'clock in the morning, on March 8, 1805.

And that, perhaps, is after all the most remarkable

GENERAL EATON AND HAMET BASHAW ON THE MARCH TO DERNE

feature of the whole affair—not that they should have arrived at Derne, but that they should ever have started. They marched, fifteen miles, twenty miles a day, tramping through the sand under the African sun, much of the time within sight of the sea, an ill assorted, poorly equipped, temperamentally incompatible, haphazard crusade, held together by some such fantastic obstinacy as occasionally animates the sons of man, by a reckless loyalty to a fortuitous cause, and by the volcanic, browbeating, dominating personality of the blue-eyed Xenophon from Connecticut. One would like to know what songs they sang, what laughter they found to share, what visions occupied their contemplation. What thoughts came drifting through the General's mind in the noonday, mirage-laden heat—of green hedgerows, possibly, and a Dartmouth Freshman, long ago, marching from Mansfield to Hanover with a pack of pins and needles, and one pistareen of money in his pocket; and now the clatter and clamor of an army with camels behind him, his saddle bags heavy with gold, and at the end of the road—what, at the end of the road?

They set out on March 8, and on March 9 the mutinies, and desertions, and tribulations occasioned by the Arabs' and camel drivers' cupidity began. "Money, more money, was the only stimulus which could give motion to the camp," Eaton wrote on the second morning, and from then on there was to be no peace. Day after day, they sat on their haunches and refused to stir unless their pay were increased, and at night they prowled through the camp, a murderous menace to the Christians, and stole everything they could reach, down to the polish on Midshipman Peck's buttons.

And at Moscarah, on March 18, only one hundred and seventy miles from the starting point, the camel drivers announced that they had not been hired to proceed any further. Eaton borrowed every additional sou he could collect, reduced his personal funds to three Venetian sequins, and persuaded them to continue for two days to a native settlement where other camels would be obtainable. The next morning, with the money in their pouches, all but forty of the camel drivers deserted, and a few hours later the remaining forty departed. The expedition was now entirely without transport, and the Sheiks decided that this would be an excellent moment to send a messenger to Bomba to find out if the American ships were there. Eaton took his marines into Moscarah Castle, cut off the rations of the Arabs and threatened them with starvation. The next day, out of a sky which may not have been as clear as it appeared, fifty camels came back, and the army moved forward again.

They arrived, on March 22, at the settlement, where they found great herds of cattle, sheep, goats, horses and camels, and three tribes of Arabs who had never seen a Christian. The Arabs were tremendously impressed, and began to enlist under Hamet's banner, bringing with them their families, tents and moveables, forage for the animals and some provisions for Eaton's men who were already reduced to bread and rice. Ninety camels were secured, at eleven dollars a hump, for the journey to Bomba. Things were going better when, on March 26, a courier arrived from Derne with the news that an army of Yusuf's was advancing on the city and would unquestionably reach it before Hamet. The camel drivers immediately vanished away to the hills with their camels, followed by one of the Sheiks with all his Arabs. Hamet himself retired to his tent and took counsel of his prudence, while Eaton stormed up and down the camp and set his marines to mount guard over the supplies.

On March 27, seeing that nobody cared what he did, the sulking Sheik came back with his Arabs. On March 28, another contingent of Arabs deserted for the day, returning, however, in time for supper. On March 30, all the Arabs decamped, with such provisions as they could seize, so that they did not reappear until April 2. Finally, on that day, Eaton called a council with Hamet of all the Sheiks, and "exhorted them to union and perseverance," in an address which can only have been a masterpiece of diplomacy, cajolery and energetic eloquence. There were now some twelve hundred people in the camp, including seven hundred fighting men—the American ships would be at Bomba—a dried fig for Yusuf and his army! Perhaps Hamet, with Eaton at his elbow, also said a few optimistic words. They marched, on April 3. Ten miles out they stopped. What now? Well, some of the Arabs had discovered that their stock of dates was running low, and the Pyramids would dance before they moved from that spot without first replenishing their supply from an inland depot five days' march distant. Eaton consigned them and their dates to the lowest Tophet, and pushed on. And on April 5 they were at Salaum on the coast, one hundred and fifty miles from Derne.

They marched again, on April 8, and almost immediately Hamet called a halt. It was, he claimed, necessary to rest the army—but it did not take Eaton long to find out that Hamet had sent a courier to Bomba to look for the American ships. In fact, the nearer they approached to Derne, and to the vicinity of Yusuf's heralded army, the less Hamet thought of this expedition, and the more the Arabs were inclined to a cautious and remunerative procrastination. But Eaton was not in a position to procrastinate. He had remaining exactly six days' rice rations and no bread or meat whatever. So he cut off all supplies and called on Hamet to march. At three o'clock in the afternoon, Hamet and the entire Arab detachment started to march—back to Salaum. They stopped, however, to seize the provisions, and before anyone knew what was happening the Christians found themselves face to face with a revolted army. Hamet had lost his temper, Eaton was rapidly losing his, the Arabs were prancing up and down, ready to charge if anybody so much as sneezed. On all sides, long, brown fingers were closing around the triggers of threatening muskets—Eaton's life was not worth one of those Venetian sequins. But Mr. O'Bannon and Mr. Peck kept their heads, Hamet's own people gathered around him and implored him not to be a fool, and to remember that the

Americans were his only hope—and suddenly it was all over. Excited nerves were calmed, Hamet dispersed his Arabs, Eaton distributed some food. Everybody sat down.

"We have a difficult undertaking!" Eaton wrote in his journal that evening, with superb reticence.

On April 10, the courier returned from Bomba with the information that the American ships were there, and empty stomachs were filled with courage. For five days they marched, a straggling, famished band down to their last grains of rice, and on April 15, with "our people scattered throughout all the plain in search of roots and vegetable substances to appease the cravings of hunger," they arrived at the Bay of Bomba.

There was not an American ship to be seen.

10

Starvation, fury, despair—of all the terrible moments in store for the expedition, there was to be none, perhaps, more dreadful than the evening of April 15 at Bomba. There was nothing to eat, there was nothing to drink, the Americans had betrayed them. Why the Americans in the camp were not slaughtered on the spot remains a miracle. They retired to some high ground, away from the Arabs who were preparing to return into the desert, and built camp fires. And at dawn the next day, there was the *Argus* coming into the Bay, followed soon after by the *Hornet*. It was quite true, the American ships had been there the previous day, but they had not thought it wise to wait any longer, and only the

glare of Eaton's camp fires had brought them back—
brought them back just in time, with food, and
water, and supplies.

And with despatches. And if Eaton had not
known before of the Government's intention to
make peace with Tripoli, he knew it now, for there
was a letter for him from Commodore Barron, written
after the receipt by the latter of Eaton's convention
with Hamet. A letter which praised Eaton's courage, energy and perseverance, and expressed the
Commodore's "ardent desire" that his most sanguine
expectations might be realized, but which reminded
him that—

"You must be sensible, Sir, that in giving their
sanction to a cooperation with the exiled Bashaw,
Government did not contemplate . . . to fetter
themselves by any specific or definite attainment as
an end. . . . You may depend upon the most
active and vigorous support from the squadron . . .
but I wish you to understand that no guarantee or
engagement to the exiled Prince, *whose cause, I
repeat it, we are only favoring as an instrument to an
attainment and not in itself an object*, must be held
to stand in the way of our acquiescence to any
honorable and advantageous terms of accommodation which the present Bashaw may be induced to
propose. . . ."

Aside from that—

"the observations which I here convey to you are
far from being intended to cool your zeal or dis-
courage your expectations, but they are what I con-

ceive necessary to make, and drawn from me by the
purest feelings of duty; and as such permit me to
recommend them to your calm and candid consideration. . . .   Much is dependent on the operation
of circumstances.   Hence the impropriety of tying
you down with positive instructions.   Many things
must necessarily occur in which your judgment and
discretion alone can be your guide. . . ."

But Eaton's judgment and discretion told him
only one thing, to march the remaining forty odd
miles to Derne and capture it, and after that no one
would dream, surely, of making peace with Yusuf
until Tripoli itself had fallen.   And so they marched,
on April 23, towards the cultivated fields of Derne,
while a herald proclaimed that—

"He who fears God and feels attachment to Hamet
Bashaw will be careful to destroy nothing.   Let no
one touch the growing harvest.   He who trans-
gresses this injunction shall lose his right hand."

On April 26, they were ready for their last few
miles, and the Arabs seized their last financial opportunity.   To a man, they mutinied and started home,
listening eagerly for the clink of the two thousand
dollars which Eaton finally shook in the ears of their
Sheiks.   And then at last, at two o'clock in the
afternoon, they were camped along the hills over-
looking Derne.   The long march was over.   And
in the strongly fortified town the Governor had
eight hundred men, and Yusuf's army was only
three days away.   Hamet "wished himself back to
Egypt," and the Governor of Derne replied, "My

head or yours!" to Eaton's proposal of surrender.
But the Arabs of that region were coming in from all
sides, until Hamet had nearly two thousand horsemen at his disposal, and, on April 27, the *Argus*, the
Hornet and the *Nautilus* arrived off the harbor.

Eaton advanced at once, while the ships were
landing supplies, artillery and marines, and at two
o'clock in the afternoon, under a heavy bombardment of the shore batteries by the squadron, the
attack on Derne became general. For a while the
resistance was most effective, but Eaton charged
with his Americans and Greeks and captured the
batteries, in a furious mêlée in which he lost fourteen
men and was himself wounded, and then Hamet and
his cavalry came swooping into the town and up to
the Governor's palace. The Governor hid himself
in a harem, from which he subsequently escaped,
and at four o'clock, for the first time in American
history, her fifteen Stars and Stripes were flying
above an old-world fortress.

Derne was captured—on to Tripoli!

II

But first there was Yusuf's army to be disposed of.
Eaton fortified himself, and wrote to Commodore
Barron that it would be unthinkable to make use of
Hamet merely for the purpose of securing a peace,
and, on May 8, the enemy arrived. There followed
days of high talk and mutual bribery, during which
Eaton refrained from accepting any "presents of
pastry, cooking, preserves or fruit" from anyone in
town, and then, on May 13, the Tripolitans attacked

in force. For six hours the battle raged up and down the streets of Derne, while Hamet and his followers fought with considerable conviction, and finally, before the steady cannonading from the ships, the enemy broke for the surrounding hills.

Yusuf's Arabs were deserting in droves, the Tripolitan army was mutinous and disorganized, Eaton was begging for money, and men, and supplies with which to push his advantage and carry the war to the usurper. The time had come, revolt was brewing in Tripoli itself, Yusuf was sitting on an anxious sofa—and then Eaton learned from his Commodore that he had instructed Mr. Lear, the United States Consul at Algiers, to open peace negotiations with Yusuf. Barron, it seemed, was extremely sick—his illness became so serious eventually as to impair his faculties for the time being—and Lear, who possessed great influence over him, had talked him into it, perhaps; or it may be that certain naval officers resented the achievements of the unpopular Eaton, that *soldier*, who, according to one of them, was winning all the honors of the war. In any case, Mr. Lear was on his way to Tripoli, and as for Hamet, the Americans had put him in Derne and from now on he must manage for himself.

Eaton was furious. It was shameful, he wrote, to make peace now with Yusuf except at the cannon's mouth, and it was little short of treachery to have encouraged Hamet so far—Eaton did not, perhaps, stop to consider how much of that encouragement had come from himself—and then to abandon him when his usefulness was at an end. And in the meantime, the hopeful, unsuspecting Hamet was careering back and forth with his cavalry, giving a good account of himself, until, on June 10, he held his ground for four hours against repeated enemy charges, in a pitched battle which brought five thousand men into the field and resulted in renewed defeat for the Tripolitans.

And Eaton may have cried with rage, for the very next day the frigate *Constellation* was at Derne. And Derne was to be evacuated at once, by order of Commodore Rodgers now in command, for peace had been signed with Yusuf, on June 4. A miserable peace, providing for a ransom of sixty thousand dollars for the imprisoned Americans, and a "consular present" of six thousand from each new official. To be sure, the word tribute did not appear in the document.

There must have been a ghastly moment, such as it is not required of many men to undergo, while Eaton realized his helpless responsibility to an entire province given over to vengeance. He could blame Lear, and Barron, and the rest of them, but in his heart he knew that his own rashly promissory enthusiasm was at fault. And then he stumbled out into the glaring streets of Derne, and walked with reluctant feet to the palace for that bitter ordeal, that personal interview with Hamet whom he had come to like so well, in spite of his little timidities and tantrums. Hamet the gentle, whom he had found that day in Tunis and set upon the road which was to lead him to a throne, and who must now be told the shabby truth. Hamet the trustful, who

had believed some words on a piece of paper in
Eaton's handwriting. It is difficult to say which of
the two men is to be the less envied as the curtains
part to confront them. . . .

12

Hamet, poor soul, does not seem to have com-
plained. He was too desperately frightened, and
his one concern was that America should not abandon
his person as well as his cause. He must be allowed
to depart with the Americans—Derne might con-
ceivably be spared, but there would be no mercy for
him from Yusuf—and in the meantime, a show of
continued hostilities must be maintained or otherwise it was more than likely that Eaton and all the
Christians would be massacred.

And so, on June 12, they drilled the troops as
usual, and even issued rations and ammunition as
if for an impending attack—and went with calm,
and perhaps smiling faces through the streets of that
town already marked for sacrifice, in the midst of
that host destined to betrayal. And if the long
weeks of the desert march to Derne had been weari-
some, the few remaining hours of hypocritical activity within its walls must have contained an eternity
of fatigue.

At eight o'clock in the evening, with as little fuss
as possible, the *Constellation's* boats came to the
wharf. The artillery, the cannoniers and the Greeks
were embarked "with silence and alacrity, but with
astonishment." When these were all safely aboard
the frigate, the boats returned for Hamet, who had

come down from the palace with fifteen chosen followers ostensibly to attend a conference with Eaton.
Silently, and swiftly, but perhaps with less astonishment, they rowed away into the darkness, followed
by the American marines. It was then two o'clock
in the morning. Alone, on the wharf, Eaton was
waiting, the last to leave the doomed city in which
men and women were sleeping quietly under the
Stars and Stripes. And then suddenly the sleeping
city awoke, there was a stirring in the houses, a
panic-stricken running through the streets, a tumult
of voices ringing through the night. The Lord
Hamet—the American fighting men—Eaton Pacha—
where were they, what was happening?

Eaton "stepped into a small boat which I had
retained for the purpose and had just time to save my
distance when the shore, our camp and the battery
were crowded with the distracted soldiery and populace; some calling on the Bashaw, some on me, some
uttering shrieks, some execrations. . . ."

Those poor people. They ransacked the camp,
and during the early hours the Arabs, followed by as
many of the inhabitants as could join them, went
flying to the mountains, taking with them every
animal, every beast of burden in the town. The
next morning, an envoy from Yusuf presented himself at the gates with a letter of amnesty if those
remaining surrendered; but they rejected it, saying
that they knew the Bashaw's perfidy too well to be
taken in by it, and that they were resolved to "defend themselves to the last moment from the terraces
and walls of their houses against his troops."

And the *Constellation* was under way, taking with her a Chieftain and his General, and the pick of his troops, and the curses of an entire populace.

"It is to be hoped," Eaton wrote as the white houses of Derne dropped astern, "the position they have taken may terminate in an accommodation and save the tragedy that menaces them. In a few minutes more we shall lose sight of this devoted city, which has experienced as strange a reverse in so short a time as ever was recorded in the disasters of war. . . . This moment we drop them from ours into the hands of their enemy, for no other crime but too much confidence in us!"

Or in himself, he had, perhaps, better have said. . . .

13

At Syracuse, where the fugitives were put ashore, Eaton served as Judge Advocate to the court of inquiry, before Captains Barron, Campbell and Decatur aboard the *Constitution*, which exonerated Captain Bainbridge of all blame for the loss of the *Philadelphia;* then, on August 6, he sailed, and arrived in Hampton Roads in November.

His name was on every tongue, the President honored him in his message to Congress, public dinners were tendered him in all the cities through which he passed—he was the Hero of Derne. Congress nearly decreed him a medal, Boston named a street after the town which he had conquered, Massachusetts gave him "a tract of land to contain ten thousand acres of any of the unappropriated

land of this Commonwealth in the District of Maine,"
half of which he sold three years later at fifty cents
an acre.   All this popularity, and the resentment
which he felt against Mr. Lear and Commodore
Barron, led him, however, into excesses of vitupera-
tive indiscretion which were not softened by those
other convivial excesses "which afterwards became
almost habitual," and during which "his egotism,
rashness and authoritative manners, excited disgust
in the minds of many."

And his accounts were not settled.   So that, after
a tour of the West in the summer of 1806, he had to
return to Washington for another session of Congress.   And still his accounts were not settled, perhaps because he talked too much about Mr. Lear
and his peace, or about the Hero of Derne and his
war.   And then Colonel Burr was arrested by a
Government which was determined at any cost to
convict him of treason, and on January 26, 1807,
Eaton made his famous affidavit against him in open
court at Washington; an affidavit which could only
have been the product of an alcoholic recollection of
debatable facts.   And in February his accounts
were settled.   Eaton put on his big hat and his
Turkish sash, and went off to the bar-room of the
Eagle Tavern, at Richmond, to attend the trial—
at the close of which Mr. Blennerhassett found that
"the once redoubted Eaton has dwindled down in
the eyes of this sarcastic town into a ridiculous
mountebank, strutting about the streets . . . when
he is not tippling in the taverns."   He had only
four years to live. . . .

And Hamet stayed at Syracuse, with his chosen fifteen, living on the allowance of two hundred dollars a month which Commodore Rodgers gave him, and writing plaintive letters to America until, in 1806, Congress was moved to appropriate twenty-four hundred dollars which finally reached him more than a year later.   But he was also writing to Eaton with whom he remained in friendly communication until the other's death in 1811, and Eaton, in his cups or out of them, was not one to forget what he regarded as the American Government's treachery in using Hamet as an "instrument" to obtain its ends and then casting him aside like an old shoe.

And so, in 1807, with Eaton clamoring in his behalf in America, and the United States Consul at Tunis exerting his influence on Yusuf, Hamet's family was restored to him; in the following year he was granted a pension by his brother, as a result of which he took up his residence in Morocco—and, in 1809, he was appointed Governor of Derne, which had, after all, been spared. Governor of Derne, and perhaps he landed at that same wharf from which he had fled in the middle of the night four years before—or perhaps he came riding in to the palace along that street which had echoed to the charging hoofbeats of his victorious Arab cavalry— and perhaps the inhabitants were pleased to see him once more. But he did not stay long, for, in 1811, Yusuf chased him out again—he may have tried to organize another uprising—and he retired in haste to Egypt where, soon after, he died. An ill fated

personage, who would probably not have made a
good Bashaw. . . .

Of them all, the irrepressible Leitensdorfer was
the most fortunate. For, having gone from Syracuse to Salona, where the Turks immediately seized
him as an apostate and put him in chains, he finally
secured his freedom from them and withdrew to
Palermo. There, temporarily, he married a third
wife, and then he took ship to America, and landed
at Salem, in December, 1809. With letters from
Eaton to the authorities at Washington, he sought
employment from the Government, and served as
a map maker, and also as a night watchman at the
Capitol, until the Senate graciously awarded him a
year's pay as a captain in the United States Army,
and a half section of land.

And Congress would have increased the grant to a
whole section, but the Senate, mindful of its recent
munificence to Hamet, and sternly conscious of its
proper obligations, refused to be carried away by
any sentimental promptings of extravagance, and
stood firm for the half section. And to Leitensdorfer it very probably seemed that half a section
of land in America was better than none at all in
Tripoli. . . .

III

Theodosia Burr, Prodigy

THEODOSIA BURR, PRODIGY

I

ON November 25, 1783, at one o'clock in the afternoon, the British troops at New York left their posts in the Bowery Lane and retired to their ships; stopping on the way, however, to grease the flagpole from which they had removed the halliards, so as to give General Washington and his entering Americans as much trouble as possible in hoisting their precious Stars and Stripes. It was Evacuation Day, and in the crowds on Broadway there may have been a baby, an infant of six months—a little girl called Theodosia Burr.

At any rate, her father and mother are almost certain to have been in the welcoming throng. The Burrs had only just come to New York, into Mr. Verplanck's house on Wall Street, before moving into a house on Maiden Lane for which they were paying two hundred pounds a year; from Albany, where the little girl had been born, on June 20, and where Colonel Burr had taken his bride after their marriage at Paramus, New Jersey, in July of the previous year. His wife was the widow of a British officer, Colonel Prevost—and there were those who looked askance at Colonel Burr for such an unpatriotic choice—and she had been Miss Theodosia Bartow, of Shrewsbury, New Jersey. At the time of her marriage to Colonel Burr she had two nearly grown sons, she was a good ten years his senior, she was not beautiful—she was, in fact, slightly disfigured—and she brought him no material fortune.

But in the estimation of her almost fanatically studious, polished and critical husband, she brought him something infinitely more worth while. For, in that age of general feminine mental vacuity, she shared with Mrs. John Adams, and not many others, a reputation for unusual brilliancy of mind and elegance of manners. She was widely read in philosophy and literature, she was a careful student of Chesterfield, Rousseau and Voltaire, she loved pictures and books. And Colonel Burr loved her, as he explained, because she had the truest heart, the ripest intellect and the most winning and graceful manners of any woman he had ever met—and the Colonel had met quite a few.

They moved, in 1785, to an elegant house on the corner of Nassau and Cedar Streets, famous for its beautiful garden and grapery, where they lived in considerable ease with a retinue of servants—one of whom, a certain Hannah, seems to have been unusually partial to the liquid products of the grapery. Colonel Burr, with Mr. Hamilton, was one of the leaders of the New York Bar, and already a member of the Legislature; the two Prevost step-sons, in whose welfare he always took the liveliest

THEODOSIA BURR
By St. Memin

interest, worked in his office; the entire household
was devoted to its fascinating master, that diminu-
tive man, with the large head and the splendidly
flashing black eyes; life passed very prosperously
and pleasantly for the little family—except for
the fact that the Colonel's activities at Albany and
elsewhere kept him so much away from home.

They all regretted these long absences, Mrs.
Burr, her two sons, little Theodosia; and that
other little girl, the mysterious, sickly Sally, concerning whom there has always been so much unnecessary speculation.

For while it has always been said that—except
for two boys who died at birth—Theodosia was the
only child of that marriage, still, the Burrs' letters
of 1785, 1786 and 1787 contain many references to
"our dear Sally," and to "our children" and "the
girls," and in 1787, Mrs. Burr was writing to her
husband that—

"Our two pledges have . . . been awake all
evening. I have the youngest in my arms. Our
sweet prattler exclaims at every noise, 'There's dear
Papa,' and runs to meet him."

The sweet prattler was Theodosia, aged four, who
already gave evidence of an attachment to her
father which was "not of a common nature," so
that she could not hear him mentioned when absent "without an apparent melancholy." The
youngest in Mrs. Burr's arms was undoubtedly
Sally; a younger sister of Theodosia, who lived for

a few years and then passed out of the family's correspondence.

"We have lost our youngest child, our Sally—a beautiful, lovely Baby," Colonel Burr wrote to his sister, Mrs. Reeve, on October 12, presumably of 1788—although, as quoted in Mr. Todd's *General History of the Burr Family*, the letter is dated 1786, no doubt as the result of a typographical error, since in 1787 Sally was still alive.

As for the two engravings by Mr. St.-Mémin— both of them frequently assumed to represent Theodosia, although there is little, if any, resemblance between them—that of 1797 was labeled by the artist "Miss S. Burr," whereas that of 1796 was marked by him "Miss Theodosia Burr." But it does not necessarily follow—in fact, the date, and the evident age of the person portrayed, make it impossible—that the "Miss S. Burr" of 1797 was Theodosia's sister; for there were many Burrs, and among them many Sallys, and this one is much more likely to have been a cousin.

2

At the age of three, Theo, as they called her—or Miss Prissy—was already the pet of the family; by the time she was ten, she had turned into a small, plump little girl, very beautiful, and not very strong. She adored her father and her big half brother Frederick; she hated cats, but had a fatal fondness for green apples; she was lazy, and full of pranks and fibs. She was quite hopeless at Arithmetic, she ran away as often as possible from her practicing at the piano forte, she spelled in a manner not sanctioned by Mr. Cheever's *Accidence* or Mr. Webster's blue backed *American Institute;* she was not particularly thrilled, probably, by the piece about "The Child trained up for the Gallows," in Mr. Bingham's *American Preceptor*, or by the uninspiring statement that "The Bee is a noble Pattern of Industry and Prudence." She was, fortunately for her, a perfectly normal, impulsive little girl.

Fortunately, because she was the child of Aaron Burr; a man descended from severe dominies and schoolmasters, himself a mental prodigy in early youth, and now possessed of an insatiable mania for the inculcation of learning. A relentless taskmaster with a passion for instruction, who seized upon his daughter and made of her a living experiment in advanced pedagogy. A stoic, too, abstemious and unemotional, who practiced fortitude and austerity, and subjected his daughter to a vigorous discipline of self control and routine—causing her, at a tender age, to sleep alone, and walk in the dark through empty portions of the house in order to dispel her childish fears; and restraining her to the simplest breakfast of bread and milk, instead of the customary hung beef, and creamy cheese, and hot bread soaked in butter.

And when it came to Theo's education, Colonel Burr was greatly influenced by his reading of Mary Wollstonecraft's *Vindication of the Rights of Women*, and determined that his daughter should be treated intellectually as though she had been a boy. At all

costs she must not grow up a mere fashionable woman
of society; he would rather that she died forthwith,
and he hoped "by her to convince the world what
neither sex appears to believe, that women have
souls."

And so, in order to demonstrate this interesting
theory, there came to Theo a host of tutors and pre-
ceptors—Mr. Chevalier, Mr. de St. Aivre, who could
not find a fiddler because even his furniture had
been seized by the sheriff, Mr. Martell, Mr. Gurney,
Mr. Hewlett, Mr. Leshlie—to teach her to dance,
and to skate, and to play the harpsichord and the
piano forte—on an elegant instrument purchased
at Philadelphia for thirty-three guineas—and to
instruct her in French, in German, in Latin, in
Greek, in Philosophy and all the kindred Arts, as
well as in the humbler fundamentals of reading,
and writing, and the troublesome "ciphering."
In vain, even Mrs. Burr protested, when Theo was
eight, that she could make no progress while she
had so many "avocations"—Colonel Burr replied
that two or three hours a day at French and arithmetic would not injure her; and during the following summer, at Pelham, the child was ciphering
"from five in the morning until eight, and also the
same hours in the evening," while her father found
it difficult, because she read so much and so rapidly,
to provide proper and amusing French books for
her—"an intelligent, well informed girl nine years
old."

In the midst of his own arduous duties at Albany,
and later at Philadelphia in the United States Sen-

ate, one can only admire Colonel Burr's ceaseless concern in Theo's progress, in every detail of her upbringing, in every moment of her daily life; his meticulous guidance and criticism of her reading, her studies, her deportment, her journal, her spelling, her handwriting—every breath that she drew. But when all is said and done, there is something rather horrifying, surely, in the spectacle of that little girl, who, at the close of her tenth year, was reading Horace, Terence and Lucian, studying Gibbon and the Greek grammar, speaking German and French, playing the piano forte and the harp, and learning to ride, to skate, and to dance.

When did she find time to make mud pies, to play with her dolls, to hop about on one foot, to shout, and dirty her face, and tear her clothes? Was she ever allowed to do any of these pleasant and necessary things?

3

In the spring of 1794, after a long, weary illness, Mrs. Burr died, of cancer. Father and daughter were drawn even more closely together—in spite of his enforced, continued absences, mitigated by an almost constant correspondence in which the solicitous, and often critical and even fretful, attitude of the parent was never for a moment relaxed. Colonel Burr was never satisfied; the child's letters were never long enough, they never came often enough, they were frequently not attentive enough to his interminable catechisms. One may read into his own epistles a father's desperate anxiety and care for an only, motherless daughter—or one may suddenly receive the disturbing impression of a cold, almost inhuman personality forever anticipating the success of an experiment which had become an obsession, and probing impatiently into its pathetic little shortcomings and failures. Had she done this, had she read that, could the next Latin lesson not be increased, did she realize that her last letter had not been fit to show to anyone. In one case, to be sure, her letter had been splendid, and he had exhibited it with enormous satisfaction, after changing a misspelled word—an extremely significant confession, perhaps. Far more than his mere flesh and blood, she was the creation of his spirit, the product of his mind in which he took so great a pride, the apotheosis of his intellect. Fortunately, again, for her, she adored him.

Theo was in her twelfth year, and now, in addition to her accumulating studies, she was become mistress of her father's home. The new city house on Partition Street, in 1795, and, later, the estate and mansion of Richmond Hill. To assist her, besides a corps of [servitors, she had the ancient and faithful Peggy, and the impeccable Alexis; and she had Madame de Senet, who also taught the harp, and the latter's *protégée*, Natalie de Delage de Volade—a little French girl whose family had been scattered by the revolutionary disaster to the household of the Princesse de Lamballe, and who was taken into the Burr establishment as a playmate for Theo.

Colonel Burr's hospitality was renowned; his

library, filled with the works of Mr. Godwin, Mr. Jeremy Bentham and Miss Burnet, was a noted one; the tall candelabra on rollers shone on the pictures of Mr. West and Mr. Copley, on Wedgwood china, and on much fine silver and cut glass. Fond as he was, especially, of French society, he gathered around him all that polished, distinguished circle of French *émigrés*, fugitives in America from the upheavals in France. At one time or another, such men as Talleyrand, Louis Philippe, Volney, Jerome Bonaparte, passed through his drawing rooms, along with Hamilton, and Jefferson, and many of the most notable American figures of the day. And always at the head of the table, doing the honors for those great ones with a dignity and charm which enthralled them, sat the little girl with the long curly hair cut in a bang across the forehead, just above the flashing black eyes.

Sometimes, indeed, she entertained in her father's absence, and even more important visitors. In 1797, for instance, when a letter of introduction from Colonel Burr presented to her the celebrated Joseph Brant, with the request that she receive him with respect and hospitality, since he was not "one of those Indians who drink rum," but quite a gentleman. Fourteen year old Theo was quite perplexed, and in particular regarding the nature of the repast which must be prepared, as she had always supposed that "savages" were cannibals; but she ended by inviting fourteen gentlemen of renown, including Dr. Hosack and the Bishop of New York, to dine in state with Thayendanegea, Captain of the Six

Nations and Chief, of the Mohawks—who came,
all six feet of him, one hopes, in full feather, and
behaved like "a most Christian and civilized guest."

It was in 1797, too, that Theo began to spend her
summers at Richmond Hill, the mansion in which
Colonel Burr had once served under General Wash-
inton, and which he had purchased a few years
before. A large, rambling, wooden house facing the
Hudson, situated on a prominent crest some two
miles from the city between Lispenard's Meadows
and the Minetta Brook at Greenwich, surrounded
by extensive grounds and lawns reaching all the
way to the river. A stately mansion, with its lofty
chambers and beautiful mahogany staircases, raising
its graceful portico of Ionic columns against a
background of splendid oaks and cedars. A mansion
built in 1760 by Major Abraham Mortier, a great
friend of Lord Geoffrey Amherst, with a long tradition of elegant hospitality within its walls; in his
time, and in that of Mrs. John Adams, who occupied it in 1789, and found it set in the midst of ven-
erable trees and fields variegated with grass and
grain, at an agreeable distance from "the noble
Hudson bearing upon its bosom the fruitful produc-
tions of the adjacent country," and enlivened by the
serenading of countless birds.

Colonel Burr had always loved the place; he
spent money on it extravagantly now, putting up
gateways, enlarging the building, planting trees and
shrubs, and widening the brook into a lake which
the villagers called Burr's Pond. And Theo loved
it too, managing her maids, and grooms and foot-

JOSEPH BRANT
From the *London Magazine*, July. 1776

men, whom she paid as much as ten dollars a month
to polish the hoofs of the carriage horses, and scrub
their teeth, and treat their coats with paste of whit-
ing; rejoicing in her gardens filled with hollyhocks,
snowballs, tulips and Jerusalem cherries; and de-
lighting in the lovely, peaceful countryside through
which she went galloping, terrifying the rustics with
her daring leaps and breakneck habits.

4

Theo was fourteen, plump, petite, rosy cheeked;
with all of her father's grace, and repose, and curious delicacy of countenance, very self assured and
positive. She was a finished Latin, Greek and
German scholar; she was reading two hundred
lines a day of Homer, and was translating French
comedies and English political treatises; she was
familiar with all the economic and philosophical
writers of the time. She was known throughout the
island, and at Albany and Philadelphia, for her dignity and charm, and for her astounding precocity,
and envied by many older belles for her fortune and
popularity. And yet one has a picture of a rather
lonely little girl, striving breathlessly to keep pace
with her father's fantastic standards, perplexed
and unhappy sometimes, so that he was obliged to
write to her in one of his more tolerant moods that—

"You must not 'puzzle all day,' my dear little
girl, at one hard lesson. After puzzling faithfully
for one hour, apply to your arithmetic, and do enough
to convince the Doctor that you have not been idle."

And the father's admonitions never ceased. If she should dine at Mrs. Penn's, "I will apprise you," he told her, "of one circumstance by a trifling attention to which you may elevate yourself in her esteem. She is a very great advocate for a very plain, rather abstemious diet in children. . . . Be careful, therefore, to eat of but one dish, that a plain roast or boiled, little or no gravy or butter, and very sparingly of dessert or fruit; not more than half a glass of wine. . . . If they ask a reason, Papa thinks it is not good for me is the best."

Theo was become his most cherished companion and counselor. In the political campaign of 1800—when Mr. Hamilton rode in vain on his white horse from precinct to precinct trying to stem the tide which was sweeping Mr. Jefferson and Colonel Burr into the presidential nomination—Theo was in the thick of the conferences between her father and his corps of young Tammany henchmen from the "Pig Pen" Tavern, the "myrmidons" of Federalist scorn, whom she proudly called the Tenth Legion. "The happiness of my life," he assured her, "depends upon your exertions, for what else, for whom else do I live?" And he continued to mould her to his will—her habits, her occupations, even her features—

"There is nothing more certain than that you may form what countenance you please. An open, serene, intelligent countenance, a little brightened by cheerfulness, not wrought into smiles or simpers, will presently become familiar and grow into habit. A year will certainly accomplish it. Your physiognomy has naturally much of benevolence, and it will cost you much labor which you may well spare to eradicate it. Avoid . . . a smile or sneer of contempt. . . . A frown of sullenness or discontent is but one degree less hateful."

5

Theo was seventeen, and there were many suitors, even without the ones which legend has ascribed to her—Washington Irving, for instance, whom it is doubtful if she ever knew personally; and John Vanderlyn, the country boy whom the Colonel befriended, with whom Theo is sometimes said to have been in love, although she was only twelve when he left the United States, not to return until after her marriage when he painted the famous portrait of her which he considered his best work in America; and a son, whose identity is not revealed, of one of the great Republican families in the state, with which Colonel Burr is reported to have sought such an alliance for political purposes.

Many suitors, probably, until young Mr. Joseph Alston, of South Carolina, came through New York during the summer of 1800, and after that there was no time for other suitors. He was the son of Colonel William Alston, one of the foremost planters and slave owners in his state; a very fine young man, twenty-two years of age, talented and extremely popular; already a member of the Bar, a great traveler and something of a poet; and the possessor of a large estate, The Oaks, inherited from his grandfather, on the Waccamaw River, in All Saints'

Parish, Georgetown County. A very fervent, eloquent young man with his soft Carolinian speech,
from that South which seemed so far away, who fell
head over heels in love with Theo and then wrote
her long philosophical dissertations about it, filled
with classical allusions and the restrained periods of
a graceful rhetoric.

For Theo did not want to marry him, oh no, Mr.
Alston; she had a sincere friendship for him, and
that was all. Charleston, she had heard, was full of
plague and excessively hot, resounding with "the
yells of whipped negroes," and its gentlemen were
absorbed in hunting and gaming while the ladies
had nothing to do except "come together in large
parties, sip tea and look prim." And when Mr. Alston had a long answer for that, Theo reminded him
that Aristotle had said that no man should marry
before he was thirty. But Mr. Alston was not interested in Aristotle.

"Hear me, Miss Burr," he begged her, at the start
of a veritable brief on the subject. "Suppose
(merely for instance) a young man nearly two and
twenty, already of the greatest discretion, with an
ample fortune, were to be passionately in love with
a young lady about eighteen, equally discreet with
himself, and who had a 'sincere friendship' for him
—do you think it would be necessary to make him
wait till thirty? Particularly where friends on both
sides were pleased with the match?"

No, Miss Burr did not really think so; already
before receiving his letter she had written "to tell
you that I shall be happy to see you whenever you

choose; that, I suppose, is equivalent to very soon. . . . My father laughs at my impatience to hear from you, and says I am in love. . . . I had intended not to marry this twelvemonth . . . but to your solicitations I yield my judgment."

They were married at Albany, where Colonel Burr was busy in the Legislature, on February 2, 1801.

They spent a week at Albany, and then went to New York alone, to dear Richmond Hill, for a few days; and then to Baltimore, where they met Colonel Burr and accompanied him to Washington City, that village in a wilderness, to see him inaugurated, as Vice President of the United States, on March 4.

And it was only by a few votes that he was not to be President, actually, in place of Mr. Jefferson with whom he had been tied as a result of the election. While the honeymooners had been at Richmond Hill—and while thousands of people come from all over the country were sleeping fifty in a room on the floors of Washington taverns, and standing in crowds in front of Conrad's boarding house on Capitol Hill to catch a glimpse of Mr. Jefferson, the "Mammoth of Democracy"—Congress had been trying to break the deadlock. With Mr. Nicholson of Maryland brought in his sickbed to be present, and with the defeated Federalists obstructing every move, the balloting began, on February 11. Nineteen ballots that day, and it was midnight and Congressmen in nightcaps were snoring all over the chamber; nine more ballots through-

out the night, and they adjourned until Friday,
took one ballot at noon, and adjourned again until
Saturday. On that day, after four more ballots,
they adjourned until Monday.

Outside, in the streets, the crowds were stirred by
outlandish rumors. Mr. Jefferson would be elected
by force; the people of Philadelphia had risen in
arms and were marching on Washington. Hours of
anxious waiting found their outlet in noisy processions singing for Jefferson and Liberty—

> "Calumny and falsehood in vain raise their voice
>   To blast our Republican's fair reputation,
>   But Jefferson still is America's choice,
>   And he will her liberties guard from invasion .   .   ."

On Monday, February 16, the thirty-fourth and
fifth ballots were taken, and then something happened. Colonel Burr had refused to pledge himself to certain Federalist measures, Mr. Jefferson had
signified his willingness. On the thirty-sixth ballot,
Maryland, Vermont and Delaware changed their
votes, and Mr. Jefferson was elected. As Mr. Bayard of Delaware wrote to Mr. Hamilton—

"I was enabled soon to perceive that he"—Colonel
Burr—"was determined not to shackle himself with
Federal principles. . . . The means existed of elect-
ing Burr, but this required his cooperation: by de-
ceiving one man (a great blockhead) and tempting
two (not incorrupt) he might have secured the
majority of the states."

The Vice President elect, therefore, and the
Alstons arrived at Washington in an uproar of bon-

fires and public jubilations, in the midst of which the Federalists were dolefully proclaiming that the Moon of Democracy was arisen, and that the Eagle of Freedom was now replaced by the Owl. And, in another great din of guns and bells, Theo saw her beloved father take his place as the Second Gentleman in the Land, and watched him escort Mr. Jefferson to his chair, in the presence of the Chief Justice of the United States, Mr. John Marshall—a prophetic juxtaposition which was to have its sequel six years later in a courthouse at Richmond.

And then the Alstons went on South; for once, it was Theo who had gone away on a journey, and Colonel Burr wrote from New York that it was dreary, solitary, comfortless and no longer home without her; and Theo wrote back and advised him to marry again, which he did, finally, in his seventies. . . .

6

There followed some happy months for Theo. She adored her husband, without for a moment forgetting her father, and while she was always to prefer northern scenes, still, "where you are, there is my country, and in you are centered all my wishes." She was very busy setting in order her two Waccamaw plantations, Hagley and The Oaks, and the summer home on Debordieu Island, and sending to New York for furniture, and apples, a cook—one wonders why, in Carolina—and a chambermaid who came, in time, with Colonel Burr's recommendation, "a good, steady looking animal aged twenty-three."

She was received with open arms in lovely Charleston, when she came there for Race Week and the Saint Cecilia Balls, to the Alston residence on King Street; and one imagines her driving in the cool of the evening on the Battery; as the youngest bride present, it may be, at her first Saint Cecilia, coming down to supper on the arm of the President; visiting in those serene Charleston mansions which turned their shoulders so diffidently to the world, preserving for their inmates the dignity of their columned piazzas and the scented shade of their precious gardens filled with jessamine, and roses, and azaleas; sitting, perhaps, of a fragrant Sunday morning, in the family pew at St. Michael's or St. Philip's, or possibly out in the country, at St. Andrew's parish church or at St. James, Goosecreek, among the pines.

In the summer when she was not at the island, she traveled, to the mountains and at the North, sometimes without her husband. To Niagara and Grand River, where she called upon the Chief of the Mohawks, who entertained her royally in his turn and gave her gifts of moccasins; to Saratoga, to Ballston Spa, into New England, and, of course, to Richmond Hill. And once, in the spring of 1802, the Vice President went South, and visited her at The Oaks; a memorable occasion, no doubt, fraught with considerable ceremonious festivity.

"My father, the Vice President of the United States . . ."

And constantly, in between times, Colonel Burr wrote to her as he had always done, advising, suggesting, insisting, criticizing, complaining, as though she had been a little girl still, and not a young married lady with her own troubles. She must not suffer any operation to be performed upon her teeth. She must walk a great deal, even without her husband, and, if necessary, "to be in form," with ten negroes at her heels; she must, for this purpose, provide herself with a stout pair of over-shoes, and the kind that came up to the ankle bone with one button to keep them on would be best, and would she write to say that she had done so. There is something rather ludicrous in all this pother of details, but the Colonel was bound to have his nose at every crack, and that was not all—

"The ladies of Philadelphia," he told her in December, 1801, "unite in the opinion that the 'energies of the men ought to be principally employed in the multiplication of the human race,' and in this they promise an ardent and active cooperation. . . . I hope the fair of your state will equally testify their applause of this sentiment, and I enjoin it on you to manifest your patriotism . . . in the manner indicated."

As a matter of fact, the boy, Aaron Burr Alston, was born in May, 1802; a "sweet little rascal," whom they took to calling "Mammy's treasure" and "the Vice President."

Theo went North with him, almost at once, to stay five months during which she wrote to Mr. Alston—"Ah, my husband, why are we separated. . . . When will the month of October come . . . it appears to be a century off"; and in 1803 again,

this time accompanied by her husband, she had the
boy at his grandfather's.   And the Colonel was
delighted with him, and called him "Gampy,"
because of his baby pronunciation of the word
Grandpa—a word which, in the little fellow's mind,
seems always to have meant Grandpa Burr, whom
he adored, and not Grandpa Alston, who may or may
not have resented the fact.   And because Colonel
Burr was utterly unable to keep his hands off any
potential pupil who came within his grasp, and
because his dictatorial mania, especially in matters
of education, had if anything increased, one finds
him writing, in 1804 when the child was only nineteen months old—

"I am sure he may now be taught his letters,
and then put a pen into his hands and set him to
imitate them. He may read and write before he is
three years old. This, with speaking French, would
make him a tolerably accomplished lad of that
age, and worthy of his blood."

The Edwards, Burr blood, of course.   And a few
months later, when "Gampy" was barely two, after
the Colonel had calmly ordered the mother to trans-
late the Constitution into French for him, he was
reminding her that if she were—

"quite mistress of natural philosophy, he"—the
boy—"would now be acquiring a knowledge of
various branches, particularly natural history, bot-
any and chymistry. . . . Pray take in hand,"
he advised her, "some book which requires attention and study. You will, I fear, lose the habit of

study which would be a greater misfortune than to lose your head."

One begins to wonder whether, for his part, the Colonel had not lost his mind in certain respects; and—as Mr. Blennerhassett was inclined, later, to believe, and Mr. Cowles Meade to be convinced— whether he was not actually slightly "deranged."

7

And this sinister aspect of Colonel Burr becomes more impressive when one realizes that Theo was, at the time, an extremely sick young woman. The birth of the boy had left her very weak—"if Heaven grants him but to live, I shall never repent what he has cost me," she told her husband. Already in 1802, she was suffering from nervous depression, and a general apathy from which she could only with difficulty be aroused. Saratoga and Ballston Spa did her no lasting good, her long journeys exhausted her, and in the spring of 1803 she was really desperately ill. Only the occasional "delightful confusion" of some domestic "bustle" seemed capable of giving "a circulation to the blood, an activity to the mind, and a spring to the spirits." She absorbed quantities of mercury, and, at the age of nineteen, wrote pitifully to Mr. Alston that—

"I have now abandoned all hope of recovery. . . . You . . . must summon up your fortitude to bear with a sick wife the rest of her life. At present my general health is very good, indeed my appearance so perfectly announces it that physicians smile at the idea of my being an invalid. The great misfortune of this complaint is that one may vegetate forty years in a sort of middle state between life and death. . . ."

So that the news, in July, 1804, that her father had quarreled with Mr. Hamilton over some exceedingly insulting letters, called him out and shot him, found her in a distressing condition.

"Oh Burr, oh Burr!" they were singing at New York—

"What hast thou done?
  Thou hast shooted dead great Hamilton!
  You hid behind a bunch of thistle,
  And shooted him dead with a great hoss pistol!"

The Vice President of the United States was practically a fugitive from justice, a coroner's jury had returned a charge of murder against him—although for just what reason, in that duelling age, is not so clear—and Theo was in a panic of apprehension, and, possibly, reproach, for he wrote her not to let him have "the idea that you are dissatisfied with me a moment. I can't just now endure it. At another time you may play the Juno, if you please."

At all events, his "dearest Theodosia"—to whom he was "indebted for a very great portion of the happiness which I have enjoyed in this life," and who had "completely satisfied all that my heart and affections had hoped or even wished"—was extremely depressed and feeble during the whole of that summer, a part of which he spent in St. Simon's Sound and in the Floridas; so that her

husband was not able to put into effect those recom-
mendations which the Colonel had addressed to him
on the night before the duel, in that amazing letter
in which he still found time to entreat him to—

". . . stimulate and aid Theodosia in the cultivation of her mind. It is indispensable to her happiness and essential to yours. It is also of the utmost importance to your son. She would presently
acquire a critical knowledge of Latin, English, and
all branches of natural philosophy. All this would
be poured into your son. If you should differ with
me as to the importance of this measure"—and the
suggestion is, no doubt, significant of some previous resentment on the father's part of the father-in-
law's interferences—"suffer me to ask it of you
as a last favor."

The Vice President resigned, after reminding the
weeping Senators that "this House is a sanctuary,
a citadel of law, of order and liberty," in which,
if anywhere, resistance would be made "to the
storms of political frenzy and the silent arts of corruption." During that summer of 1805, in which
Theo was again so sick and despondent, he traveled extensively in the West and in the South, con-
versing with many people on a variety of extraordinary subjects. And in the course of his journey he
came to Blennerhassett's Island. In the following
year he returned there, with Mr. and Mrs. Alston
and the boy.

8

It was an island in the Ohio River, at the mouth
of the Little Kenawha, a "solitary island" turned

into a "terrestrial paradise" of lawns and shrubs, pastures, fruit and vegetable gardens, surrounding a white, two storied house with curving wings, which had cost its owner thirty thousand dollars. His name was Harman Blennerhassett; an Irishman who had come to America with the "tender partner of his bosom" and two children, and a large fortune; a man "whose soul is accustomed to toil in the depths of science and to repose beneath the bowers of literature, whose ear is formed to the harmony of sound, and whose touch and breath daily awaken it from a variety of melodious instruments." Peace, tranquillity and innocence—so, moreover, Mr. Wirt was subsequently to declaim—shed their mingled delights around him. And in the midst of it all, "this feast of the mind, this pure banquet of the heart," came Colonel Burr and the Alstons.

And in a short while, according to Mr. Wirt, the whole scene was changed. Mr. Blennerhassett's shrubbery breathed its fragrance upon the air in vain, he liked it not; his ear no longer drank the rich melody of music, he preferred the clangor of trumpets; even "the prattle of his babes" and "the angel smile of his wife, which hitherto touched his bosom with ecstasy so unspeakable," left him unmoved. So it was to appear to Mr. Wirt, summing up, at the time, for the prosecution, in the case of the Federal Government against Aaron Burr.

Actually, it is difficult, even today, to determine exactly what took place. It is not feasible, certainly, in these pages to reconstruct more than the mere outline of the castle in Spain which Colonel Burr

erected upon the deluded hopes of his fascinated
followers, and of his own possibly disordered imagination.   There had, probably, been talk of a separation from the Union of the western states—no
very terrible matter at a time when the whole of
New England was roaring for a Northern Confederacy bounded by the Delaware, under the admitted leadership of a former Secretary of State—
but this project had already been abandoned.
There was a scheme, too, for the colonization of the
Washita lands in Louisiana, that fabulous region,
reputed to be full of salt mountains and giants,
which Mr. Jefferson had recently purchased for
fifteen million dollars—enough dollars, as they said,
to make a pile three miles high.   And then, *in the
event of war between America and Spain*, there was
to be an expedition into Mexico.

They were counting on that war—just as some
forty years later, in California, Mr. Frémont was
to count on a war with Mexico and not be disappointed, so that he became a hero as a result of his
escapade and not a public criminal.   And in 1806,
war with Spain seemed inevitable; many high Federal officials predicted it, Mr. Jefferson, apparently,
wanted it—until Napoleon informed him that France
would stand against him; but as late as 1807 he was
still writing to his Minister at Madrid—"we expect
. . . from the friendship of the emperor that he
will either compel Spain to do us justice or abandon
her to us. We ask but one month to be in . . .
the City of Mexico."   It is a question, indeed,
whether the President was not quite aware of the

intended expedition, and in favor of it; at all events, he had certainly been sounding out Louisiana and the Floridas as to their attitude in the event of hostilities.

And so they were preparing their floating expedition, and planning, perhaps, to seize New Orleans; and dreaming an extraordinary dream in which Colonel Burr was to be Emperor of Mexico, and his grandson Heir to the Throne, his daughter Chief Lady of the Court, and her husband Head of the Nobility; there was to be untold wealth, the fabled treasure of the Aztecs, mines of silver and gold; and Mr. Blennerhassett was to be Ambassador to England, and Commodore Truxton, possibly, Admiral of the Navy, and General Wilkinson Commander-in-Chief of the Army—a sorry figure, the latter, a former leader of the Kentucky Secession movement, and now on the payroll of Spain while in command of the military forces of the United States, a fact which Emperor Aaron I would have done well to have ascertained. A gentleman of scattered and expensive loyalties.

Colonel Burr talked and Theo smiled; Mr. Alston gave his security for the fifty thousand dollars which Mr. Blennerhassett subscribed. Proclamations were issued, secret ciphers were concocted, and many fragile promises made. The Spanish Ambassador probably smiled up his sleeve. The Alstons went home to await the "clangor of trumpets."

And then General Wilkinson decided to wash his grimy hands in Spanish gold dust. He forwarded to Mr. Jefferson, with other heroic communications of his own, an incriminating letter purporting to

THEODOSIA BURR ALSTON
By Vanderlyn

have been received from Colonel Burr—although many people, including Senator Plumer, were of the opinion that there was in it "more of Wilkinsonism than of Burrism," especially since the Colonel was noted for his epistolary reticence—in which there was reference to a "host of choice spirits," among them Wilkinson himself, and to the departure of Colonel Burr, "never to return," accompanied by his daughter and grandson, and to be followed by his son-in-law, in October, "with a corps of worthies." Whereupon General Wilkinson began to arrest people right and left, and sent an emissary to the Viceroy of Mexico with a modest request for two hundred thousand dollars, to defray his "great pecuniary sacrifices in defeating Burr's plans" and throwing himself, "Leonidas-like, in the Pass of Thermopylae"; a request which the Viceroy rejected with considerable asperity.

Mr. Jefferson—who freely admitted the practicability of Colonel Burr's venture against Spain, but was now cautiously giving heed to Napoleon's warnings, so that the projected expedition was become, perhaps, an awkward bedfellow—read the letter with great interest. He also listened to many reported rumors, and, with fascinated attention, to such fantastic affidavits as that of "General" William Eaton—a gentleman who had recently conducted an expedition of his own in Tripoli—in which that worthy stated that Colonel Burr had expressed to him the intention of turning Congress neck and heels out of doors, assassinating the President, seizing the Treasury and the Navy, and de-

claring himself protector of America. A program,
Mr. Beveridge points out, which could only have
been conceived at a time when "General" Eaton
and Colonel Burr—who seldom touched spirituous
liquors—were both gloriously drunk.

In any case, Mr. Jefferson laid the whole matter before Congress, in a Message which startled
that body and terrified the nation into a panic of
hysterical rage. Colonel Burr had committed treason,
Colonel Burr had planned to overthrow the Government, Colonel Burr had led an expedition against
the United States. There had been a "battle."
Colonel Burr's guilt, Mr. Jefferson imprudently informed the world, was "placed beyond question"—
a pronouncement which drew from Mr. John Adams
the observation that if Colonel Burr's guilt was "as
clear as the Noonday Sun, the First Magistrate
ought not to have pronounced it so before a jury
had tried him."

The first thing the Alstons knew, Colonel Burr had
been arrested, on February 19, 1807, and was being
taken to Richmond. Theo was in a fury of despair.
Some of her letters, the Colonel told her, indicated
"a sort of stupor"; she must "come back to reason"; she must "amuse" herself collecting in-
stances of virtuous men subjected to "vindictive and
relentless persecution," and write him an essay with
"reflections, comments and applications." Mr.
Alston, for his part, was not writing any essays;
he was writing to Governor Pinckney of South
Carolina, and exonerating himself as rapidly as possible of any connection with Colonel Burr's infam-

ies, of which, the Governor might rest assured, Mr. Alston had had no suspicion. His wife and child had not accompanied Colonel Burr, neither had he followed, in October, "with a corps of worthies," since they were, all three of them, quietly sitting at The Oaks watching their rice crop; and Colonel Burr had had no right to make use of his name in such a manner.

Mr. Alston was a monument of protesting indignation—he had, it may be, never actually seen further than the Washita Colony scheme, although Mr. Blennerhassett thought differently—and for once, perhaps, there was bitter discord and recrimination on the Waccamaw River. . . .

9

Already on March 30, 1807, when Colonel Burr was arraigned before Chief Justice Marshall, Richmond was a madhouse; so that it was necessary at once to transfer the ceremonies from the Eagle Tavern, where Colonel Burr was lodged, to the Hall of the House of Burgesses in order to accommodate the spectators. By May 22—when proceedings were opened before the Grand Jury in the United States Court for the Fifth Circuit and the Virginia District, in the presence of Justice Marshall and Judge Griffin—the five thousand inhabitants of that demure little town had been increased by many other thousands from all over the country, who were sleeping in tents, and in the wagons in which they had traveled, encamped along the river banks and on the hillsides. Day after day, in a sweltering tem-

perature which reached ninety-eight degrees in the
shade in June, great throngs strammed up and down
the Brick Row, shoving each other off the sidewalks as they went reeling in and out of saloons and
inns, the Eagle, the Swan, in search of the good Virginia brandy with which the proceedings of this
legal carnival were copiously irrigated.

And, of course, toiling up the hill and fighting
their way inch by inch into the court room—while a
tall, ungainly personage in frontier clothes with his
hair all over his face, who said his name was Andrew
Jackson, was making fiery speeches outside against
the 'persecutor" Jefferson—to stand on tiptoe,
and on the edges of precarious window sills, and
one young man called Winfield Scott on the great
lock of the front door itself, in order to get even a
glimpse of the little Colonel, so pale and erectly elegant in his black silk clothes and powdered hair; of
the gigantic, sprawling, untidy looking Chief Justice; of that jury containing some of the most notable citizens of Virginia under the foremanship of
Mr. John Randolph of Roanoke; of the lawyers on
both sides, fulminating acrimoniously back and
forth for the special benefit of the audience—the
prosecutor, inadequate, anxious Mr. Hay, and his
associates, that sour, belligerent, sarcastic old Lieutenant Governor McRae and the fascinating, flow-
ery Mr. Wirt; and the attorneys for the defense,
the crippled Mr. Baker, prosy Mr. Edmund Randolph, the youthful, caustic Mr. Benjamin Botts,
the great Mr. Wickham, and pugnacious, red faced,
liquidly convivial Mr. Luther Martin, "the rear

guard of Burr's forensic army," bellowing about "the dogs of war, the hell hounds of persecution."

A great mob of men, sweating, smoking, spitting into the square sand boxes or wherever convenience might dictate; gentlemen in stocks and ruffled linen, in buckled breeches and silken queues; backwoodsmen, farmers, mountaineers, frontiersmen, in long hair, and deerskin coats, and red woolen shirts; almost all of them Republicans come to see a traitor convicted, aggressively partisan, inflamed by a screaming official press, bitterly hostile to the accused, so that bondsmen for him were hard to find in the face of the public hatred which stood, clamorous and menacing, at the elbows of the jury itself and of the Court.

Fortunately, there was sitting upon the Bench, unmoved and solitary above the tumult—Judge Griffin does not seem to have contributed more than his physical presence to the scene—the calm, dominating and immeasurably courageous figure of the Chief Justice. A gentleman who had sworn to safeguard the Constitution and proposed to do so; a gentleman for whom the Law was not an instrument of party politics or of personal vengeance; a gentleman who required evidence and proof.

Fortunately, because in the background of this extraordinary trial there loomed another figure, passionate, arbitrary and endlessly cunning. A gentleman who threatened the Chief Justice with removal if he allowed the accused to escape; a gentleman who set the entire machinery of the Federal Government in motion to facilitate a condemnation, who, on his own initiative, spent more than ten thousand dollars of the public funds in the securing of witnesses from all over the Union by a drag-net process of questionnaires, who furnished his attorneys with pardons to be dangled as a bait for complaisant testimony, and with minute and continuous instructions concerning the conduct of the case, to the preparing of which he devoted the greater portion of his time; a gentleman who permitted himself to write, when the matter was before the Grand Jury, asking whether "the letters and facts, published in the local newspapers, Burr's flight, and *the universal rumor of his guilt*," were not "probable ground for presuming the facts" and placing him on trial. Mr. Thomas Jefferson, President of the United States.

Mr. Marshall, however, required proofs, not rumors. Already at the preliminary examination he announced—and his voice was intended to carry as far as Monticello if necessary—that he could not discharge the prisoner unless it was evident that there was no suspicion against him, but that this did not signify that "the hand of malignity may grasp any individual against whom its hate may be directed, or whom it may capriciously seize, charge him with some secret crime and put him on the proof of his innocence." But Mr. Jefferson had announced Colonel Burr's guilt in advance, with sensational indiscretion he had proclaimed it to Congress, and to the nation which forthwith accepted the foregone verdict as a fifth gospel—it must, therefore, be so; and it must, consequently, at all costs be established, or leave the Chief Magistrate utterly discredited and ridiculous. As against Colonel Burr himself, Mr. Jefferson had "never had one hostile sentiment"—a statement of the sincerity of which the history of their previous relations is perhaps the best indication.

And so, day by day in that seething, dripping court room, there unfolded the amazing—the dismal and at the same time inspiring—spectacle of a Chief Magistrate's vindictive prosecution of a personal enemy, embittered by his hatred of a Chief Justice who might not be intimidated, and who himself despised him. And in the midst of it all, a little man in black silk, on trial for his life. . . .

10

There can be no question, here, of discussing the legal features of that great suit, or the judicial problems involved. With Mr. Beveridge's *Life of John Marshall* before one, one may only presume to evoke a few of the dramatic moments which distinguished its course, some of the more personal incidents which enlivened its progress.

From the very first, the defense insisted, and Mr. Marshall upheld, that if Colonel Burr was guilty of treason the Government must first prove that a treasonable act had been committed, and, in such an event, that the accused had been present. In this connection, on June 9, Colonel Burr demanded that one of General Wilkinson's letters to the President be produced, and not only that, but that a subpœna *duces tecum* be issued against Mr. Jefferson, requiring him to appear in person with the document. This was a good deal of a petard for the prosecution, and they had a tremendous time over it. Mr. Luther Martin got going—would this President, "who has raised all this absurd clamor," pretend to refuse papers which might be necessary to save a man's life? If so, he was "substantially a murderer, and so recorded in the register of Heaven." Mr. Randolph got going. Mr. Hay got going. The President could not be ordered about that way. Mr. Luther Martin got going again.

"Is the life of a man lately in high public esteem," he thundered, "to be endangered for the sake of punctilio to the President?" Were "envy, hatred and all the malignant passions" to pour out their poison against a citizen and not be enquired into?

Mr. Luther Martin thought not, and the country, on the whole, thought not. At all events, Mr. Marshall issued the subpœna. In the midst of the general uproar, Mr. Jefferson called Mr. Martin an "unprincipled and impudent federal bulldog," and announced that his office did not permit him to be "bandied from pillar to post." In due course, since the President of the United States was undeniably in contempt of court, Mr. Marshall issued a second subpœna *duces tecum* against him. Mr. Jefferson was considerably alarmed this time; he refused to "sanction a proceeding so preposterous," but in his confidential correspondence with the prosecuting attorney he was full of panic-stricken suggestions—could not Mr. Marshall be induced to postpone action, was there no way of calling a truce

to all this *duces tecum* business, and if the Court at-
tempted to enforce its order the United States marshal must be told to ignore it, and he would be pro-
tected from the consequences.   But by that time
General Wilkinson's reputation had been very thor-
oughly tarnished, and the matter was dropped.

The General appeared in court on June 15—another tremendous occasion.   The "great accom-
plisher of all things," according to Mr. Randolph,
the man who was to "officiate as the high priest of
this human sacrifice," and support "the sing song
and the ballads of treason and conspiracy," whose
torch was to "kindle the fatal blaze."   He came, in
full uniform, obese, grandiloquent—strutting and
swelling like a turkey cock, so it seemed to Mr.
Washington Irving—and testified for four days,
discharging the wondrous cargo of a mighty mass
of words—Mr. Irving again—at the end of which
time he escaped indictment by two votes.   And
Colonel Burr gave him just one look of withering
scorn, which did not prevent him from declaiming
to Mr. Jefferson that Burr—

". . . this Lion hearted Eagle Eyed Hero sinking under the weight of conscious guilt, with hag-
gard Eye, made an Effort to meet the indignant Sal-
utation of outraged Honor, but it was in vain, his
audacity failed Him, He averted his face, grew pale
and affected passion to conceal his perturbation."

The General was always breaking out in a rash
of capitals.

Although a little later—after he had been pro-

jected off the sidewalk and into the middle of the
street by young Mr. Swartwout—the bibulous turkey
cock who was finally to be posted at the Eagle
Tavern as a liar, a perjurer, a forger and a coward,
was writing that—

"To my Astonishment I found the Traitor vin-
dicated and myself condemned by a Mass of Wealth
Character—influence and Talents—Merciful God
what a Spectacle did I behold—Integrity and Truth
perverted and trampled under foot by turpitude
and Guilt, Patriotism appalled and Usurpation
triumphant."

On the other hand—merciful God what a Spectacle did he not himself provide!

At last, on June 24, the Grand Jury indicted
Colonel Burr for treason and misdemeanor; he was
removed, pending the formal trial, to a suite on the
third floor of the State Penitentiary, where his
antechamber was filled with visitors, and with the
fruit, and flowers, and creams sent to him daily by
the young ladies of Richmond, whose families had
long since succumbed to the fascination of his personality and to the conviction of his innocence;
and, in July, he sent for Theo.

"I should never invite anyone, much less those so
dear to me, to witness my disgrace. I may be im-
mured in dungeons, chained, murdered in legal
form, but I cannot be humiliated or disgraced. If
absent, you will suffer great solicitude. In my
presence you will feel none, whatever be the mal-
ice or the power of my enemies, and in both they

abound. . . . No agitations, no complaints, no
fears or anxieties on the road, or I renounce thee."

II

Theo came at once, sick as she was, with her
husband and son. They went immediately to the
Penitentiary and spent the night; and there followed—if one may believe Mr. Blennerhassett who
reports having heard it from Colonel Burr—a very
lively scene between the father and son-in-law concerning the letter to Governor Pinckney, as a result
of which Mr. Alston offered to print a public reconciliation but was spared this humiliation out of regard for Theo. Two letters attacking General Wilkinson did appear over the pen name of Agrestis,
which he claimed as his own, but which Mr. Blennerhassett—who thought very poorly of Mr. Alston, and who was constantly trying to recover his
money from him—ascribed to Theo herself.

And then Theo established herself in a house in
town, and began to entertain. Dinners were all
the vogue at Richmond, especially in the houses of
the members of the Bar, and the functions given by
Mr. Marshall and Mr. Wickham, his next door
neighbor, had always been famous for the prodigal-
ity of their excellent cheer as well as the flow of wit
and good humor which distinguished them. But
Theo surpassed them all, winning more friends for
her father in one evening with her sparkling smile
than his attorneys could in a month of passionate
oratory. More friends for him, and a host of devoted admirers for herself, including Mr. Luther

Martin who went running all over the town proclaiming his infatuation.

And Theo, who so loved a "bustle," must have been very happy in the knowledge that her accomplishments, her social graces and her intellectual talents, which he had done so much to foster, were serving her father in the hour of his greatest need. They were all happy—except perhaps Mr. Alston, who gives the impression at this period of a gentleman walking on very fragile eggs—there was high talk of renewed plans and ventures, and "our little family circle has been a scene of uninterrupted gaiety . . . a real party of pleasure."

And now they were in court again, during that torrid August, spending two weeks in the selection of an admittedly prejudiced jury, but public opinion at Richmond was turning. General Wilkinson had not helped the Government's cause, and the gaudy "General" Eaton, staggering from bar to bar in a tremendous hat and a Turkish sash, posturing in every taproom and violently abusing the accused, was actually helping the defense. Colonel Burr was marching every day from Mr. Martin's house, where they kept him behind bars and padlocks, with an escort of two hundred gentlemen. The prose-cution, with an army of witnesses, was trying to establish its case.

And what was it after all, what was it that had happened on that famous thirteenth of December on which Colonel Burr was supposed to have levied war against the United States, as specified in the indictment? Well, with much hemming and hawing, there had been some boats, and "about betwixt twenty and twenty-five men," and they had come and gone with lanterns, and with this, that and the other, and there had been fires, while Mrs. Blennerhassett stood "shivering at midnight on the wintery banks of the Ohio, and mingling her tears with the torrents that froze as they fell." No, Colonel Burr had not been present. Such was the State's case. The defense moved that no "overt act" had been proved. Mr. Wickham summed up for two days, followed by Mr. Randolph. Mr. Wirt made his famous speech—"Who is Blennerhassett? A native of Ireland. . . . War is not the natural element of his mind. If it had been, he never would have exchanged Ireland for America!" Mr. Botts replied with a satire which had the entire court, including Mr. Marshall, in roars of laughter. Mr. Hay spoke for another two days. And then Mr. Luther Martin, at the crest of his intemperate powers, closed this forensic tournament.

"God of Heaven!" he exclaimed. "Have we already under our form of government . . . arrived at a period when a trial in a court of justice where life is at stake shall be but . . . a mere idle . . . ceremony to transfer innocence from the gaol to the gibbet to gratify popular indignation excited by bloodthirsty enemies?"

Mr. Marshall decided that the Government had not proved its case, and the jury delivered its reluctant verdict of acquittal. "The knowledge of my father's innocence," Theo wrote as they brought her the message, "my ineffable contempt for his ene-

mies, and the elevation of his mind have kept me
above any sensations bordering on depression."
There were tremendous parties all over Richmond
that night, and especially at Mr. Martin's; in the
taverns, hundreds of Republicans got very full,
drinking damnation to the Chief Justice. The
Alstons went home.

The misdemeanor suit ended in an even greater
disorganization of the Federal forces, but the Government had not finished. Colonel Burr and his
associates were recommitted for trial in the District
of Ohio. "After all," he wrote Theo, "this is a sort
of drawn battle." There might be no end to this
process, to this persecution which would accept no
verdict but its own. And so, while roaring mobs
were hanging him in effigy at Baltimore, and while
Mr. Jefferson was threatening Mr. Marshall with
impeachment, Colonel Burr fled, eventually, to New
York, and concealed himself in the home of Mrs.
Pollock, under the name of Edwards.

He was to sail secretly for England, on June 9,
1808, aboard the packet *Clarissa*, and for several
weeks prior to his departure, and all through the
night of June 6 before he went aboard, a "Miss Mary
Ann Edwards" from South Carolina was constantly
at his side, receiving his papers and the claims of
his countless creditors, and taking her heartbroken
farewells of the father whom she was never to see
again. Farewells, on his side, in which the old habit
of correction and criticism was even then not quite
forgotten.

He was gone for four years, wandering all over

Europe, taking with him the portrait of her by Vanderlyn which became so worn from repeated rolling;
and all during those years Theo toiled for him;
collecting such funds as could be secured; appealing—without her husband's knowledge—to every-
one she could think of in his behalf, to Mr. Gallatin,
to the new President, to her old acquaintance Mrs.
Madison; and writing to him constantly, faithfully,
and with the deepest affection.

". . . you appear to me so superior, so ele-
vated above all other men, I contemplate you with
such a strange mixture of humility, admiration,
reverence, love and pride . . . I had rather not
live than not be the daughter of such a man."

These are, perhaps, the finest, most courageous
years of Theo's life. . . .

12

In 1811, Mr. Alston was running for Governor of
South Carolina, and the equanimity of the entire
household at The Oaks must have been considerably
shaken by a letter which he received, and which
may or may not shed a cold, disagreeably brilliant
light on certain events of the past. It was from
Mr. Blennerhassett—everybody had been trying
to forget Mr. Blennerhassett—and it related to
various sums of money which that poor gentleman
had not yet succeeded in recovering.

"Having long since despaired," it began, inaus-
piciously, "of all indemnity from Mr. Burr for my

losses, by the confederacy in which I was associated
with you and him, I count upon a partial reimbursement from you. . . .

"The heroic offer you made to cooperate with your
person and fortune in our common enterprise, gave
you . . . a color of claim to that succession in
empire you boasted you would win by better titles—
your deeds of merit in council or the field. . . .
But I confess, Sir, I attached a more interesting
value to the tender you so nobly pledged of your
whole property to forward and support our expedition, together with your special assurances to me of
reimbursement for all contingent losses of a pecuniary nature I might individually suffer."

Very disturbing reading for Mr. Alston, no doubt,
but there was much worse to follow. Having already
paid twelve thousand five hundred dollars of the original fifty thousand, would he now pay fifteen thousand more, or else Mr. Blennerhassett was of the
opinion that the electors of South Carolina would
be interested to learn of candidate Alston's share in
the confederacy, of his intention of joining it at New
Orleans with three thousand men, and of the manner in which he had committed "the shabby treason of deserting from your parent by affinity and
your sovereign in expectancy," vilified him in a
letter to Governor Pinckney, and perjured himself
by denying all connection with his projects. Unless
the fifteen thousand dollars were forthcoming, Mr.
Blennerhassett would publish all his correspondence
and interviews with Mr. Alston, and the latter might
rest assured that Mr. Blennerhassett had no intention of abandoning "the ore I have extracted . . .

BLENNERHASSETT ISLAND

from the mines both dark and deep, not indeed of Mexico, but of Alston, Jefferson and Burr."

But Mr. Alston did not pay the fifteen thousand dollars, the famous book did not appear for the time being, and, in 1812, he was driven to his inauguration in a coach drawn by four white mules; with Theo, no doubt, at his side, thinking, perhaps, of another inauguration.

And in the spring of 1812, Colonel Burr returned to America. He landed at Boston, notified Theo whom he intended to visit, and, in May, slipped quietly into New York. Nothing happened. Socially he was still an outcast, but his practice returned to him, the future seemed secure. For once, there was a little peace, and a prospect of happiness. And then he received two terrible letters from The Oaks. "Gampy" was dead, at Debordieu Island, of the fever.

"One dreadful blow has destroyed us. . . . That boy on whom all rested . . . he who was to have redeemed all your glory and shed new lustre upon our families—that boy at once our happiness and our pride—is dead. We saw him dead . . . yet we are alive . . . Theodosia has endured all that a human being could endure, but her admirable mind will triumph. She supports herself in a manner worthy of your daughter."

And Theo's heartbroken sentences—

"There is no more joy for me. The world is a blank. I have lost my boy. . . . May Heaven, by other blessings, make you some amends for the noble grandson you have lost. . . . Of what use

can I be in this world . . . with a body reduced
to premature old age, and a mind enfeebled and bewildered. Yet . . . I will endeavor to fulfill my
part . . . though this life must henceforth be to
me a bed of thorns. . . . He was eleven years
old . . .''

13

Theo was desperately ill, listless, comfortless.
Colonel Burr insisted that she come North. The
Governor was not permitted by law to leave the
state; Mr. Timothy Green was sent down, therefore, to escort her—an old gentleman with some
medical knowledge, whose presence was somewhat
resented at The Oaks. In his opinion Theo was too
feeble to undertake the journey by land—the Colonel
would find her very emaciated, and a prey to inces-
sant nervous fever—he took passage for her, consequently, in a schooner-built pilot boat, which happened to be refitting at Georgetown.

She was the privateer *Patriot*, Captain Overstocks, a famous vessel noted for her speed. She
had discharged her privateer crew, hidden her
guns underdeck and probably painted out her name,
and was preparing for a dash to New York, richly
laden with the proceeds of her raids. These matters were doubtless well known in the taverns where
the former crew were spending their bounty money.
The Governor, for his part, was afraid of two things:
the pirates and wreckers—the dreaded "bankers"—
who infested that coast, and the British fleet cruis-
ing off the Capes, for the *Patriot* was a valuable
prize. The pirates he could not guard against, but

to Captain Overstocks he gave a letter for the British Admiral, requesting free passage for the ship bearing his sick lady.

They went aboard, Theo, her maid and Mr. Green, with all her trunks, and, it may be, a special present for her father; a portrait, perhaps—to replace the old worn one—fresh and new, carried separately in its frame? One would give a great deal, too, to know whether there was a little black and tan dog on board. Mr. Alston accompanied her down Winyaw Bay, and left her at the bar—with many misgivings, poor soul—at noon, on December 30, 1812. Early in January—but this was not known until much later—the *Patriot* fell in with the British fleet off Hatteras, presented her letter and was courteously given free passage. That night a terrific storm arose; the *Patriot* was never heard from again.

For a few weeks they hoped against hope, while Colonel Burr walked pathetically up and down the Battery at New York, waiting for the *Patriot*, for a rescuing ship, for some word. But thirty days were "decisive." Mr. Alston was convinced that his wife was either "captured or lost." And rumors of capture were all the time reaching Colonel Burr— something dreadful had happened off that sinister Hatteras coast—but he refused to believe them. If Theo had been captured "she would have found her way to me."

"My boy—my wife—gone both!" Mr. Alston wrote in February. "This, then, is the end of all

the hopes we had formed. You may well observe
that you feel severed from the human race. She
was the last tie that bound us to the species. What
have we left . . ."

Nothing—except another letter, to Colonel Burr
this time, in April, from Mr. Blennerhassett, who
was not so soon to be put aside. He had not
yet been reimbursed, and it seemed to him very
probable that nothing short of the publication
of his book, "hitherto postponed only by sickness,"
would bring him any part of the balance due him
from Governor Alston.

"His well earned election to the chief executive
office of his state," Mr. Blennerhassett continued,
"and your return from Europe will . . . render
the publication more effective . . . I would still
agree to accept . . . $15,000 . . . and of course
withhold the book, which is entitled *A Review of the
Projects and Intrigues of Aaron Burr, during the
years 1805, 6, 7, including therein as parties or priv-
ies, Thos. Jefferson, Albert Gallatin, Dr. Eustis, Gov.
Alston, Dan. Clark, Generals Wilkinson, Dearborn,
Harrison, Jackson and Smith, and the late Spanish
Ambassador, exhibiting original documents and correspondence hitherto unpublished, compiled from the
notes and private journal kept during the above period
by H. Blennerhassett, LL.B.*"

A fascinating title, and an absorbing work, no
doubt, well worth fifteen thousand dollars; but its
publication seems to have been unaccountably
delayed, and on September 10, 1816, Mr. Alston
himself died, and was buried with his son in the

family burying ground at The Oaks under that
stone which bore the record, now, of three such
untimely deaths.

And now, for the lonely old man at New York,
there was nothing left. Yes—some relics of Theo's
which they had sent him; some lace, and a little
satinwood box, and a black satin embroidered one
with a pincushion, and a letter which he found
among her papers. A letter intended for her husband after her death, but which Mr. Alston never
saw, because he never had the courage to look at
her things, but left them, untouched, in her room
in the big house on the Waccamaw. A tragic letter
written long before, in 1805, when she was twenty-
two; a heartrending letter to read in 1816, with its
revelation of the invalid, anxious, miserable years
that had followed.

"Whether it is the effect of extreme debility and
disordered nerves," she had told him, "or whether
it is really presentiment, the existence of which I
have often been told of and always doubted, I cannot tell; but something whispers me that my end
approaches . . .

"To you, my beloved, I leave my child, the child
of my bosom. . . . Never, never listen to what
any other person tells you of him. Be yourself his
judge on all occasions. He has faults, see them and
correct them yourself. . . . I fear you will scarcely
be able to read this scrawl, but I feel hurried and
agitated. Death is not welcome to me; I confess it
is ever dreaded. You have made me too fond of life.
Adieu, then, thou kind, thou tender husband. Adieu,
friend of my heart. May Heaven prosper you, and

may we meet hereafter. . . . Least of all should I murmur . . . whose days have been numbered by bounties, who have had such a husband, such a child, such a father. . . . Speak of me often to our son. Let him love the memory of his mother, and let him know how he was loved by her. Your wife, your fond wife, Theo."

And the postscript—

"Let my father see my son sometimes. Do not be unkind towards him whom I have loved so much, I beseech you. . . . If it does not appear contrary or silly, I beg to be kept as long as possible before I am consigned to the earth. . . ."

14

Theo was dead, but the memory of her could not die, and the rumors lived.

Rumors of piracy, of mutiny, of Carolina wreckers. The *Patriot* had been captured by the celebrated pirate, Dominique You; she had been captured by the infamous "Babe"; Mrs. Alston had walked the plank with the entire ship's company. Rumors, persistent rumors; and then, twenty and thirty years later, confessions; deathbed confessions of sailors, scaffold confessions of executed criminals—mutiny, piracy, murder, a terrible dawn after a terrifying night, and a haunting picture in their minds of a lovely, gentle lady who perished very bravely and with infinite dignity. But in one version the executed criminals—two sailors at Norfolk who recur in all the stories—claimed to have been members of a gang of wreckers, on Kitty Hawk,

who had looted the *Patriot* and killed her passengers
after they had come ashore on those dreary sands.
And it is this last version which one is tempted to
remember.

And then, in 1850, a more detailed story, probably not an entirely truthful one, but connected in
many significant respects with the past, and with
what was to come in the future. So that here, at
last, whatever the antecedent events and the exact
locality, one may be in the very presence of Theo's
last ordeal. The story of "Old Frank" Burdick,
an old man reputed to have been a pirate, who, at
the time of his death, insisted that he had been one
of the crew of a pirate ship which had captured the
Patriot. He himself had held the plank for Mrs.
Alston, who walked over the side very calmly, all
dressed in white, after begging them to send word to
her father and husband. Her eyes were closed, her
hands were crossed upon her breast, and as she
took the final step she waved them as if in farewell.
She came to the surface of the waters once, they saw
her face again, and then the outstretched arms, the
hands still waving as they sank. Perhaps, for a
moment at the rail, no man spoke or dared to raise
his eyes; or perhaps they laughed, and went about
their business.

As for the *Patriot*, they had plundered her and
then abandoned her under full sail. In the cabin,
"Old Frank" remembered, there was a portrait of
the lady, and somewhere aboard a little black and
tan dog. One wonders about that little dog—why
was he not allowed to come aboard the corsair to

which all the prisoners had been transferred?—one wonders, until one realizes that the entire episode of the piracy *at sea* was perhaps a fabrication of "Old Frank's" to protect men still living on land, at Nag's Head, near Kitty Hawk just north of Hatteras—Nag's Head, a famous stronghold of the wreckers.

And so one comes, in 1869, to Nag's Head, where a certain Doctor Pool was summoned professionally one day to the house of a Mrs. Mann; a very old lady who had formerly been the wife of one of the Tillett boys, who, with the Manns themselves, belonged to the aristocracy of the wrecking "bankers" of that coast, in the early decades of the nineteenth century. In the parlor of Mrs. Mann's cottage was a portrait which aroused the doctor's curiosity; a portrait painted on wood, in a plain gilt frame, of a beautiful young woman elegantly dressed in white, in the style of 1810; a frail young woman with dark hair and piercing black eyes.

In answer to the doctor's eager questions, but with infinite reluctance and possibly many deliberate reticences, Mrs. Mann told the story of the portrait. "During the English war," when she was quite a young girl and while Tillett was courting her, a pilot boat had come ashore on Kitty Hawk in a storm, and the men had gone out to her. When they returned, they reported having found a nameless, empty ship, with her sails set and the helm tied down, and the only living creature aboard a little black and tan dog. The cabin, they said, was in great confusion, trunks broken open, and a lady's effects—some beautiful lace, some silk dresses, a vase of wax flowers—helter skelter on the floor. Hanging on the wall was the portrait. In the distribution of spoils, Tillett had claimed it for his sweetheart, along with the dresses and other feminine objects—things which Mrs. Mann showed to Doctor Pool, but the existence of which in her possession her younger sister, at a later date, had never been aware of; things which Mrs. Mann had kept hidden, just as she probably concealed many details which young Tillett may have told her about the doings that day on Kitty Hawk. Gruesome details which explained, perhaps, why the little black and tan dog was the only living creature aboard, not when they found the ship, but when they *left* her.

For while Mrs. Mann's account agrees surprisingly with "Old Frank's" story concerning the *Patriot*, one must remember two circumstances. That the *Patriot* had just passed through the British fleet, so that she would scarcely have been attacked in such a neighborhood; and that in the terrific storm which arose that same day no act of piracy on the sea can have been possible, no transferring of prisoners, no walking of the plank. One can only surmise that, if Mrs. Mann's pilot boat was the *Patriot*, she was driven ashore on Kitty Hawk during the tempest, with all her passengers aboard, and that they met their death in that place at the hands of the wreckers who swarmed out to loot her. Just as the two convicted "bankers" confessed some thirty years later.

And the pilot boat on Kitty Hawk may well have

been the "schooner-built pilot boat" *Patriot*, for the
painting in Mrs. Mann's cottage is believed by many
to have been a portrait of Theodosia Burr Alston—
the " first gentlewoman of her time," and the most
unfortunate. . . .

IV

Edmond Charles Genêt, Citizen

EDMOND CHARLES GENÊT, CITIZEN

I

IN 1820, two years before her death, an old lady
of nearly threescore and ten sat in her home at
Mantes, in France, and wrote a letter to her nephews
and nieces in America. Some thirty years before
she had seen their father, her only brother, for the
last time; more recently she had been the mistress
of an extremely elegant boarding school for young
females, on the early roll of which had been in-
scribed the names of Mademoiselle Hortense de
Beauharnais, a Queen to be, and the daughter of
Josephine Bonaparte; of Miss Eliza Monroe, daughter of the American Minister to France; and of the
Misses Pinckney, daughters of yet another American Envoy. Young ladies who paid their board in
American gold, and caused the struggling little acad-
emy to prosper, and grow into the famous establishment of more than one hundred pupils, the school-
room of Duchesses and Queens.

Now, in 1820, at the close of her life, she thought
of those boys and girls whom she had never seen, and
prepared for them a little history of their family in

France. With it she sent the letter; such a letter as
aunts wrote, once upon a time, to their nephews and
nieces.

"My dear children," she told them, "an enormous distance separates you from a large family
by which, in spite of your absence, you will always
be held most dear.

"When you look at the map of the Universe, you
see on it old Europe, and in this old Europe, France,
from which you are descended through your most
estimable father. The station which your family
occupied in France, the worthy things which they
have done and the disastrous misfortunes which they
have been obliged to bear, everything which concerns them, should interest you, and time can only
increase this interest.

"The most widely separated families may some
day, through a change of fortune, be reunited; too
frequently those tender bonds of close relationship,
loosened with each successive generation, vanish
entirely. I wish therefore, with foreseeing tender-
ness, to strengthen and maintain those bonds by
informing you, not only of the origin of your father
through his father and mother, but of the present
condition of a family which, when it was deprived of
the support and counsels of your estimable father,
experienced a loss greater than all those to which it
has been subjected as a result of the events of the
last century. Your Aunt."

The nephews and nieces in question were the children of Cornelia Tappen Clinton, and of Martha
Brandon Osgood—daughters, respectively, of the
late Vice President of the United States and of the
Postmaster General—and their estimable father was

EDMOND CHARLES GENET

Edmond Charles Genêt, one time Minister Plenipotentiary of the French Republic "at" the United
States.

2

At Christmas time, in 1762, Marie Anne Louise
Cardon Genêt was about to bring into the world her
ninth, and last, child. The two only sons had died
in infancy; it was ardently hoped that the baby
would be a boy. With this hope in her heart, Louise
Genêt retired to her canopied bed one night and
dreamed that the Virgin had come to her, bringing
a handsome boy baby in a beautiful white cradle.
The next morning she vowed that if the dream came
true the child should wear nothing but white for
the first five years of his life. On January 8, 1763,
the boy was born, in the Parish of Saint Louis, at
Versailles; and not until his fifth birthday did he
lay aside the little white suits, the white shoes and
the white hats, with which his pious mother had
filled his wardrobe. A little boy in white, in a great
house on one of the cavernous streets of solemn Versailles; Edmond Charles Genêt, destined to become
the representative of the Republic, One and In-
divisible.

It was a family of magistrates and officials, tracing
its present prosperity to the little boy's grandfather,
Jean Genêt, who, in 1702 at the age of twelve,
walked from his home near Tonnerre, in Burgundy,
to Paris, with the intention of restoring the dimin-
ished family fortunes. At Paris he attracted the
benevolent attention of the Cardinal Alberoni,

Prime Minister to Philip V of Spain, who took him to Madrid. Jean Genêt returned to France with all the religious severity of Spain in his nature, and with a fortune of four hundred thousand *livres* in his pockets, which he invested in real estate and in the purchase of a magistrature. He married, in 1721, a lady of ancient, though penurious, lineage, who gave him two sons—Edmé Jacques, the father of the little boy, and Pierre Michel, who grew up to be a recluse, a bachelor and quite sickly.

As a young man, Edmé Jacques had an adventurous time of it. Brilliant in his studies, a lover of the classics, of history and of languages, he desired to become a diplomat. His father destined him to the magistrature. When Edmé Jacques betrayed a taste for poetic composition his father nearly had him locked up in a monastery on a *lettre de cachet.* Edmé Jacques was very much in love with the beautiful Louise Cardon; his father wished him to marry another lady whose face was no part of her otherwise considerable fortune. It was thought best, finally, to allow him to travel, with the understanding that he was not to return until he had put from his mind all of his personal diplomatic and matrimonial notions.

Edmé Jacques was twenty; he would not, under the French law, attain his majority until he was twenty-five. He went to Louise Cardon and exchanged with her vows of immutable fidelity, and then for five years he traveled; in Germany, and in England, where he boarded with the Governor of Dover Castle. Dover was very near France,

Edmé Jacques slipped across one night, concealed himself for two days in the house of a friend, sent for his mother, and visited his Louise. Then he returned to Dover to await his coming of age. That was in 1751. In January, 1752, without his father's consent, he married Louise, and shortly after the birth of their first child, Henriette, he was appointed Secretary Interpreter at the Ministry of Foreign Affairs.

They moved to Versailles where, during the next six years, he borrowed on his patrimony and was blessed with six children, only two of whom survived infancy, Julie and Adelaïde. Then, in 1759, the Duc de Choiseul enlarged his bureau at the Ministry and increased his salary. He prepared, after another sojourn in England in 1762, a report on the British Navy which earned the favorable notice of Louis XV. His wife presented him with another daughter, Sophie, and with the white-clad boy, Edmond Charles. The great days of the Genêt family were at hand.

3

Edmond Charles, as he grew up, saw them in all their splendor. His father was a man of elegance and wit, a distinguished linguist, and a scholar; his house was the meeting place for all the learned and artistic world of Versailles; in its salons there were recitations, and music, and philosophical discussions in many tongues; one heard there a constant setting forth of stately matters, in the midst of a continuous passing to and fro of courtly personages, under the brilliant glow of many candles. One by one—as they left their English and Italian governesses, their piano forte, harp and singing teachers, their French poetry and elocution lessons— Edmond Charles's sisters were called to the Court and made great marriages, arranged and dowered by royal patronage.

Henriette, already Reader to Mesdames, the Daughters of the King, found herself at seventeen the chosen companion of the little fifteen year old Dauphine, Marie Antoinette of Austria; and, four years later, Her Majesty's First Lady of the Bed chamber. Julie, who sang divinely, became Cradle Rocker to the Children of France—one of them a little boy who was never to be King—and when she married M. Rousseau, in 1771, Louis XV ventured to remark that never in his experience had he seen so handsome a bridal pair. Her husband was Chamberla into the Comtesse d'Artois, Fencing Master to the Dauphin, and Cloak Carrier to the King. He was, not unnaturally, guillotined, in Messidor of the Year II. Adelaïde was also very beautiful, and a great favorite of Marie Antoinette, who appointed her Lady in Waiting, and gave her a costly present of diamonds at the time of her marriage to a gentleman who was Quartermaster General to the Army, Receiver General of Finances, and of the Duchy of Bar and Lorraine. Even Sophie, who was not at all beautiful, was made Lady in Waiting to the little Madame, Daughter of the King.

Days of splendor, bright with the sunshine of countless royal favors; but the ones which Edmond

Charles enjoyed the most were those summer days
of real sunshine when they all went rolling out, bag
and baggage, to visit Uncle Toto—Pierre Michel,
the brother of Edmé Jacques—at his country retreat
at Mainville. For at Mainville there were woods,
and birds, and cows, and a great romping, after the
solemnities of Versailles; and in the evening, Uncle
Toto with his flute, playing *Charming Gabrielle* and
My Merry Shepherd.

And Uncle Toto himself, so fond of his scamper-
ing nephew; such a simple, absent minded, gentle,
kindly old soul; so removed from the world that he
was to find it necessary, in 1793, to write to his niece
Henriette and ask her—

"Just exactly what is the Revolution? Why all
this uproar? For what reason are all these people
being put to death?"

4

At the same time, Edmond Charles's education
was most carefully planned and developed. At
the age of five, he could already read English and
recite his Greek roots. Two years later, in addition
to the instruction in history and in law which he
received from his father, he was studying ancient
and modern languages with two tutors, and learning to ride, to fence, to dance and to play on the
piano forte, an instrument for which he showed
considerable aptitude. At the age of twelve, the
amazing child was given a gold medal by the King
of Sweden for his translation from Swedish into
French of the *History of the Reign of Eric XIV.* In

the following year, he produced his translation of the *Researches concerning the Ancient Finnish Race.*

And during that period, in 1777, he helped his father in the preparation of his periodical, *Anglo-American Affairs*, translating for him into French the occasional contributions submitted by a certain Mr. Franklin, and his associates of the American Commission—splendid personages, in the eyes of the young translator, gentlemen who had come from across the Atlantic, and who talked magically of a strange, fascinating thing called Liberty.

So that it must have been with a quite special delight that, in 1779, he put on his uniform of a Lieutenant in the Colonel General's Regiment of Dragoons, and accompanied the corps to Brest, to embark for the American war. But it seemed at the last moment that there was no need of cavalry over there, and when the troopers returned to Paris, Edmond Charles remained at Brest to collect English and American nautical phrases to put into a dictionary for the use of French sailors; a task which was followed by a sojourn at Nantes, for the purpose of studying commercial and merchant shipping affairs, including, no doubt, the legal status of privateers.

It was in 1780. Edmond Charles was seventeen, he spoke several languages, he was grounded in the law, he understood the fundamental principles of commerce, he rode well, he fenced with skill, he danced gracefully, he possessed agreeable musical talents and elegant manners, he looked extremely attractive in his handsome uniform. It was time to initiate him into the diplomatic career to which he was obviously destined. He was sent to Germany, to the University of Goettingen, then to the Embassy at Berlin, later on to the Embassy at Vienna. He returned to Paris just in time to attend the state funeral of his father, the much beloved and respected Edmé Jacques, in September, 1781.

Edmond Charles was almost immediately appointed to succeed his father at the Ministry of Foreign Affairs, and it was to him that the courier bearing the first news of the surrender at Yorktown presented himself. Edmond Charles was barely nineteen. He commanded a salary of forty thousand *livres;* he had under him a staff of eight interpreters, all of them much older officials whom he treated with faultless tact. "Never, for a single moment, did he forget himself," his sister Henriette remembered afterwards. At home, he set himself to the liquidation of his father's numerous debts, and not until the last penny had been paid, several years later, did he discard the simple black attire of his mourning. Very young, very correct, very modest, the personification of integrity.

In 1783, he accompanied the special mission to London, for the negotiation of the new commercial treaty, and during his stay in England those tastes which were to claim the leisure of his later years began to manifest themselves. For the youthful Secretary avoided the gayeties of the Court; he preferred, instead, to visit the manufacturing centers, to occupy himself with scientific enterprises, to investigate the latest progress of invention; there was a

serious strain in him, a certain lofty detachment
from the frivolities which encompassed him, a great
curiosity concerning the novelties of the age.

When the States General convened, after his
return to France, for the purpose of discussing be-
lated economic reforms in the kingdom, Edmond
Charles read a report of his own preparation before
one of the committees presided over by the Comte
d'Artois. The report condemned a proposed stamp
tax, pointing out the recent English experience
with a similar measure, and greatly displeased the
Comte d'Artois; but the Marquis de Lafayette applauded the young man's courage—not in the presence of the King's brother, to be sure—and told
him that he was very young, but that he had behaved like a man. At all events, he had incurred
the displeasure of Monsieur, and it was not long
before Edmond Charles's bureau at the Ministry
was discontinued, and its duties absorbed by other
departments, ostensibly for the sake of economy.
There was a vacancy at the Embassy at St. Petersburg; Edmond Charles applied for it, and, in 1787,
set out on the long journey to Russia.

5

At Warsaw, he committed possibly his first indiscretion. At any rate, he betrayed the simmering
blood in his veins, the jealous, brash if one will,
rebellious quality of his youthful attitude towards
any disparagement of his importance as a representative of France; and, perhaps more than that
already, his impatient scorn of men whose natures

THE BATTERY, NEW YORK CITY, WITH THE FRIGATE "EMBUSCADE"

By Drayton, 1793

were not attuned to his own swift, vigorous, forward
moving instincts, and to his own deep, ceaseless
absorption in the furtherance of what they called
in France the "public concerns."   A very earnest
young man, imbued with zeal, saturated with energy,
extremely meticulous of his dignity, which was,
after all, his country's.   And at Warsaw he found
Poniatowski, King of Poland on sufferance; a
gentleman who was very fond of French operettas,
and who sat Edmond Charles down at the piano
forte and made him sing for him by the hour—until
finally Edmond Charles sang a song which the King
of Poland did not relish, so that he had the piano
forte removed, and the refrain of which ran—

> "Is he King or isn't he King?
> If he isn't, why call him King?"

At St. Petersburg, Edmond Charles found the
Empress, Catherine II—who stared at him very
hard in his dragoon uniform because of his striking
resemblance to her late favorite, the Count Landskoy
—and the Comte de Ségur, the Ambassador, who—
while he was to record subsequently in his memoirs
that Edmond Charles was extremely hot headed—
wrote of him at the time of his sojourn in Russia
that he was a very distinguished young man, in all
respects suitable, uniting agreeable talents with
profound knowledge, erudite without pedantry,
bright without pretension, his logic sound, his zeal
indefatigable, his wit ornate, his manner of thinking
noble and attractive.   In fact, the more Mr. de
Ségur became acquainted with him, the more he

found him a treasure to sustain and employ. Edmond Charles was promoted to the rank of Captain, and appointed Chargé d'Affaires when Mr. de Ségur went home, in October, 1789. That, at the same time, the young dragoon who so resembled Count Landskoy pleased the Empress, is manifest from the fact that she adorned him with diamond knee buckles.

And then most extraordinary events began to take place in France. In 1790, the King swore to maintain a Constitution; a royal gesture which left the Empress Catherine, for one, extremely unimpressed. The French Minister of Foreign Affairs instructed all his representatives to adhere to the Constitution, and then confidentially advised them to do no such thing. The King put his tongue in his cheek, and the Princes decamped from France. Edmond Charles obeyed his official instructions with alacrity, and ignored the confidential footnote. Now that it was done, he found himself Constitutionalist to the core—it was the dawn of Liberty, it was what Mr. Franklin had talked about, it was the first step down that road which the young American Republic had opened to all enlightened, right thinking men. It was glorious.

When he was not busy sending despatches about the activities in Russia of the emigrated Princes to the Foreign Minister who never opened them, Edmond Charles told the Empress that it was glorious. The Empress, very soon, began to speak of him as an insane demagogue. The emissary of the Princes thought that he was merely a "crazy little fool."

It is quite possible that Edmond Charles, in his fierce enthusiasm for the new "public concerns," made himself vocally conspicuous to a degree which deafened the despotic ears of his imperial patroness. Catherire II was very fond of good-looking dragoons —she was very fond always of Edmond Charles and did her best to persuade him to renounce France and accept a position in the Russian diplomatic service—but she forbade him the Court, as representing a monarch who was now, in August, 1791, the prisoner of his people, and surrounded him with spies. Edmond Charles reminded her tartly that he represented France, Constitutional France; he refused to become involved in the intrigues of the Princes; and he sat down to write a very fine letter to his sister, Henriette.

"My dear sister," he informed her, "I am aware of your respectful and deep attachment to your august mistress; those sentiments entirely control your actions; they are praiseworthy and should not be altered.

"My position is different from yours; a citizen of France, charged with the honor of representing my country, I must do so in accordance with the laws prescribed by the Constitution which the King has sworn to maintain, and in support of which I have also given my oath. Never speak to me in your letters of the opinions which divide Frenchmen, who would be happy if, like myself, they realized that the welfare of their sovereign and of their country resides only in the maintenance of the Constitution!

"An advanced sentinel, I remain here ready at all times to give warning of any conspiracy against my country. I do so with all the more zeal, because I believe myself to be serving the real interests of my sovereign. Place my letter at the feet of the Queen; I think it necessary that it be through you that she be made aware of the resolve to which my sentiments as a French citizen and my profound and respectful devotion to the true interests of my sovereigns alike constrain me."

The Queen read the letter and expressed the opinion that while she feared that it might hinder Edmond Charles's future advancement in the royal service—she was herself, at the time, a prisoner in her own palace—still it proved him to be a man of sincerity. And in that she was right. Edmond Charles was no barefoot *sans culotte* with nothing to lose, trailing his vociferous republicanism through the royal apartments. He was the son of an intensely royalist family, nurtured in a tradition of unswerving loyalty to his sovereigns, beholden to them for his own position and the prosperity of his sisters— two of whom, Henriette and Adelaïde, were only to escape death on the fatal August 10, 1792, as a result of his foresight in asking the protection of the Assembly for them. When he chose to uphold the Constitution, to take his stand with the patriots against his King, to break with all the training of his childhood, and splash a discordant crimson across the whole white background of his life, he did so deliberately, sincerely and with the utmost moral courage, because he was filled with admiration for the founders of American liberty, and because his reason, his instinct and his conscience left him no other choice. He was in this, surely, altogether admirable.

It was inevitable that Edmond Charles should be dismissed from Russia. His political opinions were not compatible with a continued sojourn at the Court of the Empress Catherine, and he was given his passports, in July, 1792.

"Hasten to come to the capital," the new Foreign Minister wrote to him, "where I will see you with great pleasure, since I destine you for a new mission in which I am sure you will acquire new rights to the gratitude of your fellow-citizens."

Edmond Charles passed through Warsaw, where Poniatowski was no longer King, and arrived at Paris, in October, 1792.

6

There were tremendous changes at Paris. The royal family was imprisoned at the Temple, Edmond Charles's sisters had fled with their mother to Julie's country place at Beauplan—Henriette and Adelaïde after the terrible day of August 10, on which they had stayed at the Queen's side until the last moment, and received from the King some of his most personal private documents; the Genêt fortune was destroyed.

Edmond Charles himself was most cordially received by the moderate Girondist group in power. He was made Colonel and proposed as Ambassador to Holland; he went on an important mission to Switzerland; he moved in the most select republican circles, an intimate of Brissot, Condorcet, Roland and his distinguished lady. When there was question of banishing Louis XVI, Edmond Charles was suggested as a suitable escort to conduct him to America. With this object, among others, in view, "the civic virtue with which Citizen Genêt has accomplished the various missions entrusted to him, and his known devotion to the cause of Liberty and Equality," so they officially informed him, "have decided The Executive Council to appoint him Minister Plenipotentiary from the French Republic at the Congress of the United States of Northern America." At the *Congress*, be it noted, distinctly specified.

And while Robespierre and the "Mountain" roared that the selection was founded on Brissot's personal friendship and not on merit; and while the aristocratic Gouverneur Morris advised Mr. Washington that the new Envoy looked like an upstart and possessed more genius than ability—Madame Roland wrote that the appointment was eminently deserved, that Genêt—one must begin to call him Genêt now—that Genêt was a man of sound judgment and enlightened mind, combining amenity and decency of manners; that his conversation was instructive and agreeable, and free from pedantry and affectation; and that his chief characteristics were gentleness, propriety, grace and reason. Gentleness, propriety, grace and reason. . . .

The Revolutionary scene was unfolding. Genêt witnessed the session of the Convention at which the Girondists, overawed by the Jacobin "Mountain,"

voted for the execution of the King. He went to
Beauplan to make his farewells to his family. His
mother, his sisters whom he was never to see again.
Henriette, who had not yet started her famous
school, Julie, Sophie—poor Adelaïde, the Queen's
"little lioness" who had held the door at Versailles
against the mob, and who was so soon to commit
suicide rather than be sent to the scaffold for having
given twenty-five *louis* to Marie Antoinette on the
day of her arrest. His little niece Aglaé, who was
to become the wife of Marshal Ney.

On January 23, 1793, Genêt started for Brest,
to embark on the frigate *Embuscade*. At the gates of
Paris they stopped him and searched even his trunks,
because of a rumor that he had the little Dauphin
with him. For a month he was detained at Brest by
contrary winds, and then, finally, he left France,
forever.

7

And in America many curious events were taking
place.

The country had gone solemnly insane over the
French Revolution, and was expressing its hysterical delight in that event in a series of ridiculous
republican mummeries. One talked about the Hydra
of Despotism, the Phœnix of Freedom, and the Gallo-
Columbian Fraternity of Freemen, and drank toasts
proposing that the sister republics of France and
America be as incorporate as light and heat. The
National Gazette greeted the death of Louis XVI
with the dignified observation that "Louis Capet

has lost his Caput"; and men, women, and children at half price, stormed the waxworks of the execution, at Philadelphia, to see "the knife fall, the head drop, and the lips turn blue." In the theaters, audiences sang the *Marseillaise* and the *Ca Ira*, while they watched performances of *The Demolition of the Bastille* and *Helvetic Liberty, or the Lass of the Lakes.*

At Charleston, at Philadelphia, at New York, at Boston, everywhere, they held "grand civic pageants" to celebrate the French victories. Functions attended by city and state officials, in a great to do of booming guns and clanging bells; at which *Te Deums* were chanted, and feasts consumed in halls decorated with broken crowns and scepters, and the Ox of Aristocracy paraded through the streets, accompanied by citizens in white frocks— "while the balconies of the houses exhibited bevies of our amiable and beautiful women, who by their smiles and approbation cast a pleasing luster over the festive scenes," and added their fervent soprano to the singing of republican odes setting forth that—

> "By hell inspired with brutal rage
> Austria and Prussia both engage
> To crush fair freedom's flame;
> But the intrepid sons of France
> Have led them such a glorious dance
> They've turned their backs for shame."

At Philadelphia, Mr. Washington was, of course, still President, and wishing that he were not; Mr. John Adams, who wrote books about the vile mul-

titudes, was Vice President; General Knox was
Secretary of War, and "Sandy" Hamilton Secretary
of the Treasury; Mr. Edmund Randolph, whom Mr.
Jefferson called the poorest chameleon he had ever
seen, was Attorney General; timid little Mr. Madison was leader of the House of Representatives;
Mr. James Monroe was never very far away.

And Mr. Jefferson was Secretary of State, in his
red, waistcoats and untidy woolen stockings. A
gentleman who had recently returned from a five
years' sojourn at Paris, with a mind steeped in the
fumes of a frenzied democracy, so that he reeled
intellectually in a haze of rabid republicanism
illuminated by the beacon, the "pole star" of
his self-confessed, fanatical devotion to France. A
gentleman—it is Alexander Hamilton writing—who,
together with Mr. Madison, was filled with a
womanish attachment to France, and a womanish
resentment against Great Britain; who, in France,
had seen government only on the side of its abuses,
and had drunk deeply of the French philosophy in
religion, science and politics; who had come from
France in the moment of fermentation which he
had had a share in exciting, and in the passions and
feelings of which he shared both from temperament
and situation; who had come "probably with a too
partial idea of his own powers, and with the expectation of a greater share in the direction of our
councils" than he was enjoying; who had come
"electrified plus with attachment to France, and
with the project of knitting together the two countries in the closest political bands."

A gentleman of flexible principles—the opinion is
that of Mr. Oliver Wolcott—who practiced the arts
of political chicanery with an address and perseverance such as few men had ever attained; who, in
his office, was distinguished for "an attention to all
those trifles which attend the minds of half learned,
dreaming politicians and superficial scholars." A
gentleman who imagined monarchist plots behind
every door; who listened eagerly to evil reports concerning his friends and associates, and who wrote
them down in vicious little secret diaries; who
concurred hypocritically in the deliberations of his
colleagues, and attacked them scurrilously, and
anonymously, and under the mask of venomous hirelings, in his *National Gazette*. A gentleman who, whatever the extent of his undeniable contribution to the
national welfare, was also to lend himself to many
unlovely stratagems. A gentleman obsessed with
dangerous ideals, immersed in hazardous abstrac-
tions, possessed of perilous virtues.

And for his consideration, and that of his fellow
Cabinet officers, there arose, in April, 1793, a question of great moment. There was a new French
Minister on his way to America—he arrived actually on April 8—and France was suddenly at war
with England. Should the treaties of 1778 with
France be upheld? There were two of these—one, a
treaty of alliance in which the territorial integrity of
the contracting countries was guaranteed; the other,
a pact of amity and commerce, whereby, among
other clauses, each nation might take into the ports
of the other the prizes captured by its privateers,

whereas the captures made by the privateers of other nations were forbidden entry into the ports concerned. There was also extant, though not immediately due in full, a debt of two million three hundred thousand dollars, the balance of the French loan to the United States. With France at war, and her West Indian colonies exposed to capture, loyal adherence to the treaties could only plunge America into conflict with England, and probably with Spain —and there would be an end, for one thing, of American commerce, if not eventually of American independence. The merchants were in favor of neutrality, the people at large faithful to "France and Liberty." The Cabinet must decide.

Mr. Hamilton came out for neutrality, in name and fact, and for a repudiation of the awkward treaties made with a government now no longer in existence. Mr. Jefferson desired peace—he was, perhaps, the first of America's great practicing pacifists—but under no consideration would he permit the President to declare a genuine neutrality. Such a course would be an insult to France, and with his rare capacity for riding two horses at once in opposite directions, Mr. Jefferson was determined to enjoy the benefits of neutrality without subscribing openly to the principle. Harried and bedeviled by his two great hostile counselors, Mr. Washington finally issued a proclamation, on April 23, in which no reference whatever was made to the subject of neutrality, all citizens being enjoined, merely, against committing belligerent acts.

Mr. Jefferson, Secretary of State, immediately

attacked the proclamation with all the private
weapons at his command. It was unconstitutional
because the legislature had not been consulted; it was
pusillanimous because it did not feature America's
friendship for France; it was not a "manly neutrality," but only an English one.   'Our proceedings,"
he wrote, "towards the conspirators against human
liberty"—meaning the English—"are unjustifiable in
principle, in interest, and in respect to the wishes of
our constituents."   The people, he was convinced,
were coming forward to express those wishes, since
the Government failed to represent them. An interesting observation, from a Federal official who was
so soon to be shocked by an alleged "appeal to the
people" on the part of the new French Minister.

As for the *National Gazette*—Mr. Jefferson's *National Gazette*—

"Had you, Sir," it roared at Mr. Washington,
"before you ventured to issue a proclamation which
appears to have given much uneasiness, consulted
the general sentiments of your fellow citizens, you
would have found them from one extremity of the
Union to the other firmly attached to the cause of
France. You would not have found them . . . so
far divested of the feelings of men as to treat with
'impartiality' and 'equal friendship' those tigers
who so lately deluged our country with the blood of
thousands, and the men who generously flew to her
rescue and became her deliverers . . .

"I am aware, Sir, that some court satellites may have
deceived you with respect to the sentiments of your fellow citizens. The first magistrate of a country, whether he be called a King or a President, seldom knows the

real state of the nation; particularly if he be so
much buoyed up by official importance as to think
it beneath his dignity to mix occasionally with the
people. . . . Let not the little buzz of the aristocratic few and their contemptible minions . . .
be mistaken for the exalted and general voice of the
American people."

It was in such an America, animated by such public dissensions, that the new Minister from France
set foot.

8

The frigate *Embuscade*, with her thirty-six guns,
her Liberty Cap at the foremast head and her quarter galleries decorated with the emblems of the
Terrible Republic, arrived at Charleston on April 8,
1793. It had originally been her intention to proceed to Philadelphia, but contrary winds and the
rumored presence of two British frigates turned her
aside to the Southern port.

The young man on her quarterdeck, resplendent
in the tri-colored ribbon of his ministerial office, was
exactly thirty years and three months old. A very
handsome young man, with a fine, open, laughing
countenance and a ruddy complexion, active and
full of bustle, pleasant and unaffected, "more like a
busy man than a man of business." A young man
of parts, of great culture, and of long diplomatic
experience; an admirer, since his childhood, of the
founders of American freedom; fresh from the magnificent and transfiguring ordeal of his own country's
republican rebirth, aflame with patriotism and lofty

resolves, dedicated to the constant service of France
—the new, glorious, triumphant France of his
Girondist ideals—and through her, inevitably, to
the service of the whole Brotherhood of Man.

"The whole of the new world must be made free,"
he once wrote, "and the Americans must help us in
this sublime task."

An apostle, a crusader of Liberty, come with
exalted hope to that land where Liberty had been
born, to find, surely, a concern equal to his own in
the welfare of the sister, the daughter republic.
An eloquent young man, so filled with zeal, so
dreadfully in earnest, so proud of his mission, so
sternly convinced of its sanctity and righteousness,
so fiercely confident of success. So one seems to see
him, on the quarterdeck on that April morning, and
not as the vainglorious, arrogant, blustering mountebank of history. Impatient, hot headed, petulant,
fanatic, a good deal of a spoiled child, perhaps a
little too precocious, too unabashed, too arbitrary—all of these things—but not a fool, not an
adventurer, not without conspicuous and ingratiat-
ing qualities, and never ridiculous. If he was to
offend, the reason was, in his own words—

". . . that a pure and warm blood runs swiftly
through my veins; that I passionately love my
country; that I adore the cause of Liberty; that
I am always ready to sacrifice my life for it; that
to me it appears inconceivable that all the enemies
of tyranny, that all virtuous men, should not march
with us to the combat; and that when I find an injustice is done to my fellow citizens, that their inter-

ests are not espoused with the zeal which they merit,
no consideration in the world can hinder either my
pen or my tongue from tracing, from expressing my
grief. . . ."

He was coming to take his place as a successor to
Ministers who, in the opinion of Mr. Moreau de
Saint-Méry, had proved most unsatisfactory—one
of them, indeed, having been so tactless as to cause
French dishes to be carried with him to the house,
whenever he dined at Mr. Hamilton's. He was coming to assume a position in which he would need—

"to be extremely affable, to see everything, to hear
everything, to note everything without affectation,
and without panic, to play his diplomatic rôle at
his board, to attract to it cleverly the influential
members of the House of Representatives and of the
Senate, and never to permit the British Ambassador
to serve at his table a brand of Madeira superior
to his own."

He had already been warned by the Ministry of
Foreign Affairs of the coldness of the American
character; and advised to employ indirect methods
of approach, to *exert all possible influence on the
public sentiment*, to avail himself with circumspec-
tion of the zealous cooperation of certain friends
whom he would find in the House of Representatives
and among the principal executive officials, and to
place entire confidence in Mr. Washington, in Mr.
Madison, and in Mr. Jefferson—advice which may
possibly have been responsible for his subsequent
exclamation that—

"America is so little understood in France!"

He brought with him explicit instructions, covering a number of important matters, which, as they were almost all to be repudiated by the Jacobin Government after the fall of the Girondists who had issued them, deserve to be recorded in some detail; more especially since the utmost which can be stated in condemnation of his conduct in America is that he obeyed the spirit as well as the letter of his instructions, and came within an ace of succeeding— Mr. de Saint-Méry thought six weeks.

He was to avoid as much as possible "those ridiculous disputes which cluttered up the transactions of the older diplomacy"—and there, at least, he was to fail miserably. He was to negotiate a new treaty of amity and commerce, to replace those of 1778; and in the meantime he was to insist on the maintenance of the existing agreements; to prevent any armament of privateers other than French ones, and any harboring of prizes except those taken by French vessels, in the ports of America; and to make use of the three hundred blank letters of marque furnished him by the Ministry of the Navy, for distribution to all American ship owners "willing to risk a raid against the English, the Dutch, the Russians, the Prussians and the Austrians." Even a person of less intelligent imagination than he possessed would have appreciated the tacit, underlying hope that America might be persuaded to join France in her English war.

And then he was to attempt the realization of an extraordinary dream, a vision of colonial empire, a

THOMAS JEFFERSON   Unfinished water-color sketch by Robert Field

Original in the possession of the New York Historical Society.

carrying of the banners of Liberty through Canada
and the Spanish Americas, just as on the other side
of the water the armies of France were sweeping
them across Europe. Trusting in the hostility
towards Spain of the American frontiersmen—and
ready to defray the necessary expenses for intoxicat-
ing stimulants, since it was known "that Americans
only talk of war when *vis à vis* with a bowl"—they
told him at Paris to dispense the blank military com-
missions which they had provided for the Indians,
who thought highly of such documents; and to do
all in his power, in Louisiana and the provinces adjacent to the American borders, to "quicken the principles of freedom and independence," or, in plain
French, to maintain agents in those regions for the
purpose of recruiting armed bands and stimulating
insurrection.

And if the American Government ever made up
its mind to it, he was to negotiate still another
treaty—

"A national pact in which the two nations would
mingle their commercial and political interests, and
establish an intimate harmony for the purpose of
favoring in every way the extension of the Kingdom
of Liberty, guaranteeing the sovereignty of Peoples,
and punishing the Powers which still persevere in
an exclusive colonial system. . . . This pact would
soon lead to the liberation of Spanish America, to
the opening up to the inhabitants of Kentucky of
the navigation of the Mississippi, to the deliver-
ance of our ancient brothers of Louisiana from the
tyrannical yoke of Spain, and, possibly, to the placing in the American Constellation of the bright star

of Canada. However vast this project may seem, it will be easy of execution if the Americans so desire, and in convincing them of this fact the Citizen Genêt shall exercise all his care. . . ."

Such, "with absolute trust in his known prudence and moderation," were the stupendous undertakings confided to that young man of thirty, standing on the quarterdeck of the frigate *Embuscade* while she boomed her salute to the port of Charleston.

9

The official details of Genêt's activities in America, his acrimonious debates with the Federal Government, his undeniably caustic attacks on the President, his incontestable breaches of diplomatic conduct—these matters are all to be found in the archives of formal history.

It is well known that he instigated important military and naval operations against Canada and Spanish-America; that he encouraged recruiting within the borders of neutral America; that he armed countless privateers, with fascinating republican names, in every American port, and caused their prizes to be confiscated in American courts; that he did all in his power to precipitate the United States into war; that, in short, he obeyed his instructions. It is quite true that his consuls, the captains of his frigates and their crews, permitted themselves outrageous impertinences, and indulged in riotous communion with their English colleagues in every waterfront tavern; that he called the President—

"This old Washington, who greatly differs from him whose name has been engraved by history, and who does not pardon me my successes—"

That he roared bitter and impolite complaints at the Cabinet; that he thought less than nothing of Mr. Hamilton, Mr. Randolph and General Knox; that he issued tempestuous and extremely bombastic manifestoes for the public consumption; that he made a great deal of noise, and offended a great many people, and finally frightened Mr. Jefferson out of his coat.

What is not so true is that he did anything contrary to the proper conception of his duty, to the just interpretation of America's existing obligations to France, to the widespread and loudly expressed popular approval of his point of view; what is not so well known, perhaps, is how he was secretly encouraged in his attitude by Mr. Jefferson, and how he was finally betrayed and discredited because he had become too dangerous to both American political parties. It is these matters, more particularly, which one is tempted to examine. . . .

Genêt went ashore at Charleston, after his forty-five days at sea, in a great din of guns and bells, and was received with great cordiality by Governor Moultrie, by Mr. Izard, who had known his father at Paris, and by the French Consul, who rejoiced in the name of Michael Angelo Bernard de Mangourit. From them, between the courses of various civic feasts, he learned that the Government would probably declare for neutrality—it did so two weeks later—that the people were very generally opposed to the Government's policy, and that it was perfectly proper for him to arm privateers in American ports.

Genêt did not waste any time. "I am more anxious to succeed," he wrote, "than to shine publicly." During the ten days of his stay at Charleston, he manned two privateers, saw the *Embuscade* start on her raiding voyage to Philadelphia, and set in motion the machinery of his Spanish ventures which he left in the energetic hands of Mr. de Mangourit. Then, on April 18, he started north by land, choosing a route which would take him through a countryside the farming population of which was none too well disposed toward the Federal party in power, with its unpopular excise laws, and where he might have opportunity to purchase necessary supplies of grain for the French colonies. His progress was a continuous triumph, a tumultuous ovation of guns, bells, public addresses, civic feasts and Fraternal Hugs.

"The people," he was able to report, "received me in their arms and under their modest roofs, and offered me much grain and corn. I was clasped in the arms of a multitude which had rushed out to meet me. My journey has been an uninterrupted succession of civic festivities."

Philadelphia was all bubbling over with excitement in anticipation of his coming.

"May we not hope," the *National Gazette* suggested, "that the true Republicans will hoist the tri-colored flag; and to complete the spectacle, that our fair Philadelphians will decorate their elegant

persons and adorn their hair with patriotic rib-
bands?"

Along the roads, horsemen were posted to bring in
the news of his approach; and citizen Bompard of
the *Embuscade* had agreed to fire three shots in con-
firmation of the event.

Genêt arrived at one o'clock on the afternoon of
May 16. A large concourse of citizens had marched
out to Gray's Ferry to meet him, and escort him in
triumph into the town, but he avoided them and
drove through cheering streets to the City Tavern,
at Second near Walnut; an establishment similar
to the Tontine Coffee House at New York, where all
the business of the port was transacted, and where
punch was served at side tables. Of all the conflict-
ing reports of his entry, one prefers the one tucked
away in a New York gazette, quoted from a private
letter written by a lady in Philadelphia to a Friend
in Alexandria.

"Mr. Genêt's address is so easy, affable and pleasing," she said, "that he fascinates all who have the
honor to be introduced to him. He was quite over-
come with the affectionate joy that appeared in
every face on his arrival. It would be impossible, my
dear, to give you any idea of the scene. It was great
and interesting in the highest degree. The streets
were crowded, and the city was in a tumult of joy."

On May 17, he was waited upon by deputations
of prominent citizens and replied from his balcony
to their acclamations of welcome. On May 18, he
was formally, and in his estimation a trifle coldly,

received by the President, and a little shocked to
find "medallions of Capet and his family" in the
parlor. On that same evening he attended the first
of several festivities in his honor; a tremendous
banquet at Oeller's Tavern, at which many distinguished Philadelphians, as well as some of the crew
of the *Embuscade*, were present. A banquet enlivened by odes, and hymns, and toasts—"the Treaty
of Alliance with France, may those who attempt to
evade or violate the political obligations and faith
of our country be considered as traitors, and consigned to infamy!" A banquet which closed with
the passing from head to head of a Liberty Cap,
after Genêt himself had charmed the assemblage by
singing:—

> "Liberty! Liberty! Be thy name adored forever;
> Tyrants, beware, your tottering thrones must fall;
> One interest links the free together,
> And Freedom's Sons are Frenchmen all!"

Governor Mifflin and Genêt went home at half
past nine, and the next morning the French Ambassador turned eagerly to his various tasks. While the
belles of Philadelphia—who, according to Mr. de
Saint-Méry, were adorable at fifteen, faded at
twenty-three, decrepit at forty, and afflicted with
bad teeth, falling hair and a passion for ribbons—were
promenading fashionably on the north side of Market Street, between Third and Fifth; while the
gentlemen of the town—one continues to quote Mr.
de Saint-Méry—were sitting late at afternoon din-
ner, in dining rooms furnished with maple and horse-

hair and glittering with superfluous silver, consuming
vast quantities of claret and Madeira, and retiring
occasionally to the corners of the room for purposes
which may best be imagined; while the good citizens, "who washed their faces and hands with care,
but never their mouths, seldom their feet, and even
more rarely their bodies," were smoking, and drinking
very hot tea, and devouring green fruit in that busy
city infested with bedbugs and flies; and while the
oyster barrows were being trundled through the
streets until ten o'clock at night, "with lamentable
cries"—the Citizen Minister toiled, and planned,
and organized.

He saw to his growing squadron of privateers;
he maintained that since the treaties forbade the
enemies of France to fit out raiders in American
ports the permission for France to do so was obviously intended, and that if French privateers were
allowed to bring their prizes into American harbors they might also condemn them there; he asked
for advances on the two million dollar debt and was
told by Mr. Hamilton that there was no money in
the treasury, and that even if there were he would
not receive any of it; he sent agents to Louisiana,
he incited the Canadians, he armed the Kentuck-
ians, and gathered together a fleet; he wrote vol-
uminously on a multitude of subjects, and answered
that letter concerning the Spaniards from George
Rogers Clark, which began—

"Sir, the contest in which the Republic of the
French is actually involved against all the despots of

Europe is among the most awful, interesting and
solemn, in all its consequences, that has ever arisen
in the world. . . . With those who already feel or
know anything of the Rights of Man it is a spectacle which, between hope and fear about its success, must engage the attention of both head and
heart, and with them influence every of the nobler
passions. . . ."

Soon he could inform his Government that—

"True Americans are at the height of joy. The
whole of America has risen to acknowledge in me
the Minister of the French Republic. I live in the
midst of perpetual feasts; I receive addresses from
all parts of the continent. I see with gratification
that my way of negotiating pleases our American
brothers and I am led to believe, Citizen Minister,
that my mission will be a fortunate one from every
point of view."

Cheerful, sanguine, deluded young man that he
was. . . .

10

He had every reason to be sanguine. On all
sides—excepting in purely Federalist circles—in
poetry and prose, he was being told that his cause
was just, and that the American people were behind
him. Repeatedly, at Philadelphia, riotous crowds
went storming down the streets, threatening to pull
Mr. Washington and Mr. Adams out of their beds
if they refused to make war on England. Within a
fortnight of his arrival, some of the most prominent
citizens of the town waited on him to ask his opinion

THE GOVERNMENT HOUSE
New York City

concerning a name for a new Republican club. Genêt suggested that it be called the Democratic Society.

On May 30, the Democratic Society of Pennsylvania was organized with a constitution and circular notice drafted by the Secretary of State of the Commonwealth, Mr. Alexander J. Dallas. It seemed that the events of the French and American Revolutions had taught the founders,

"no longer dazzled by adventitious splendor, or awed by antiquated usurpation, to erect the temple of Liberty on the ruins of palaces and thrones. . . . The seeds of luxury appear to have taken root in our domestic soil; and the jealous eye of patriotism already regards the spirit of freedom and equality as eclipsed by the pride of wealth and the arrogance of power."

The Society was established, therefore,

"to cultivate a just knowledge of rational liberty, to facilitate the enjoyment and exercise of our civic rights, and to transmit unimpaired to posterity the glorious inheritance of a free republican government."

Other cities were not slow to imitate the capital. At Boston, the Freemen declared that they adored the cause of Liberty, and that their wishes and prayers were frequently engaged against the Despots of the Earth. They were persuaded "that the present struggles of the French people are directed to the subversion of Aristocracy and Despotism, and to the lasting improvement and happiness of the human race." Other Societies announced that they favored a "real and genuine Republicanism, unsullied and uncontaminated with the smallest spark of monarchical or aristocratic principles."

Under the mask of abstract republicanism, it was not long before the Societies—those nurseries of sedition, as the Federalists called them, with their "barefaced correspondencies and resolves"—began to attack the administration, the policy of neutrality, and all the Federalist measures; while, on their side, the *National Gazette*—Mr. Jefferson's *National Gazette*—and Mr. Bache's *General Advertiser* were slinging criticism and abuse at Mr. Washington, until he raged against them openly at Cabinet meetings.

In the Charleston Society, which had actually affiliated itself with the Jacobin Club at Paris, they could only lament "the amazing want of Republicanism which now forms a conspicuous trait in the character composing the highest officers in the Federal government"; they resolved that war was inevitable, that the French treaties must be upheld, and that the cause of France was America's; and they believed that—

"for any man or set of men, either in private or public, and particularly those to whom the welfare of our community is entrusted, to advocate doctrines and principles derogatory to the cause of France . . . or in support of the base measures of the combined Despots of Europe, particularly Great Britain, is a convincing manifestation of sentiments treacherous and hostile to the interest of the United States, and well deserves the severest censure from all true republican citizens of America."

Genêt might tell Dr. Logan, out on the beautiful lawn at Stenton which he often visited, that he would never suffer a gazette to enter his house; but he read them just the same, and sent clippings home to France; he knew what a large proportion of the American people were thinking and saying; he found ample justification for his estimate of—

"the ardent and sublime love of the good country people, of the old soldiers, of the poor but industrious men of the cities, for the principles of France," and of "the base idolatry of the great capitalists, of the big merchants, for the English constitution."

II

And, at the Department of State, he found Mr. Jefferson.

The two men talked, not as officials, but openly and intimately as friends. Mr. Jefferson was made aware of Genêt's Spanish enterprises, and assured him that he did not care what insurrections were incited in Louisiana, although expeditions from Kentucky might prove embarrassing to the participants if captured. Mr. Jefferson thought that Genêt could not have been more affectionate or more magnanimous. Mr. Jefferson, in those early days, seemed disposed to second the French point of view, he sympathized with the French Envoy in all his disputes with the Federal Government, and, in the security of their personal conversations, disparaged the motives and pronouncements of his executive colleagues.

"He gave me," Genêt reported, "useful information concerning the men in power, and did not conceal from me that Senator Morris and Secretary of the Treasury Hamilton, devoted to the interests of England, exercised the greatest influence on the President's mind, and that it was only with the greatest trouble that he was able to counteract their efforts."

Mr. Jefferson, exposed to the hatred of the President and of his colleagues—so Genêt was given to understand the situation—was the only official for whom he, Genêt, possessed any respect.

At the same time, when it came to discussing practical details—the maintenance of existing treaties or the formulation of new agreements—Mr. Jefferson was extremely vague. He blandly admitted the validity of the French treaties, and, simultaneously, assured the British Minister that America proposed to remain vigorously neutral. He took refuge in a haze of general technicalities, and declaimed copious extracts from various tomes on international law. All in the same breath, he played the cat to Genêt's mouse, cajoled his English colleague, and succeeded in placing the public blame for the Government's spineless vacillations on Mr. Hamilton and his "secret antigallomany." Depending on the listener, he talked lengthily and with the utmost apparent sincerity, on both sides of the same question, content if in so doing he could in any degree embarrass and obstruct his enemy at the Treasury Department. As for the effect on the listener, Mr. Jefferson, treading the tortuous path of his own destiny, was not in the least concerned in such insignificant consequences of his policy.

Genêt began to realize the duplicity confronting him. Mr. Jefferson constantly said one thing and did another, he made use of "an official language and a confidential language"; in the former he publicly upheld the actions of the Government, in the latter he privately encouraged Genêt to disregard them and his own hypocritical approval of them. Mr. Jefferson, Genêt found out, "signed his name to what he did not believe, and officially approved threats which he condemned in his private conversations and anonymous writings"; there was in his official declarations "a restraint" which convinced Genêt "that this man of half-hearted convictions wished to maintain himself in a position which would keep him in office, whatever the turn of events."

But at first Genêt realized none of this. He listened to Mr. Jefferson—just as many long years afterwards the French people were to listen to another great American spokesman—and believed, as did his compatriots of that later day, that he was listening to the voice of America.

12

And now things were not going so well.

"Seeing myself upheld by the American people," he was soon to write, "I believed that a government sprung from it would prove itself worthy of its trust by obeying its supreme voice. I had not in the least foreseen that the men charged by the people with the

task of government would betray their duty by mul-
tiplying in our path obstacles, difficulties and dis-
appointments."

At all events, in June, the President proclaimed
that all privateers being armed in American ports
should be seized. During the first days of July, it
was brought to the attention of the authorities at
Philadelphia that the brig *Petit Démocrate*, ex *Little
Sarah*—a former French prize—was being armed
and made ready for sea. Governor Mifflin was re-
quested by the merchants of the port to call out
the militia and prevent the departure of this vessel
whose identity as a privateer of Genêt's was an
open secret. Governor Mifflin sent his Secretary of
State, Mr. Dallas of the Democratic Society, to interview Genêt. A very famous interview, as it turned
out, at which no one except the two men was present.
Genêt lost his temper, talked extravagantly about
his wrongs, and refused to countermand the brig's
departure. Governor Mifflin called out his militia.
In the Cabinet, sitting without Mr. Washington,
who was at Mount Vernon, Mr. Hamilton and
General Knox urged that guns be mounted on Mud
Island to sink the *Petit Démocrate* if she sailed in
defiance of the proclamation. Mr. Jefferson implored them to leave everything to him, and went
off to interview Genêt himself. Once again, Genêt
lost his temper, and shouted at Mr. Jefferson for a
long time before the latter could get in a word—
"but he did not," Mr. Jefferson recorded in his
diary, "on that, nor ever did on any other occasion

in my presence, use disrespectful expressions of the President."

It was Genêt's contention that he had a perfect right, according to the treaties, to arm privateers, and that Congress was bound to see that the treaties were observed. Mr. Jefferson told him no, that was for the President to do. Then, Genêt enquired, if the President decided against the treaty, *to whom was the nation to appeal?* Mr. Jefferson—who was upholding his Chief that evening—explained that under the Constitution the President was the last appeal. Genêt bowed and said that he could not make him any compliments on such a constitution; he might also have asked Mr. Jefferson why, then, he had attacked the President's neutrality proclamation, on the ground of unconstitutionality. After that Genêt regained his good humor, and they discussed the brig. Mr. Jefferson begged him not to allow her to sail before the President returned. Genêt informed him that she would drop down to Chester to take on supplies, and that she would probably not be ready to sail before the President returned.

Mr. Jefferson went running back to the Cabinet and reported that everything was arranged and that the brig would certainly not sail. Governor Mifflin called in his militia. Ten days later, the brig sailed —the promise that she would not do so never having existed except in Mr. Jefferson's imagination.

Mr. Washington returned to Philadelphia, on July 11, in a state of extreme impatience. Genêt asked Mr. Jefferson for an interview with the President and was told that all communications must pass through the Secretary of State. Notwithstanding this refusal, Genêt called at Mr. Washington's house that same evening, and, "after some very polite and obliging discourse on the part of Mrs. Washington," persuaded the President to give him a few moments in private. Genêt "protested what is entirely true"—his account was written four years later—

"that I had been entirely amazed on reading in the public journals certain articles which they attributed to me, relative to his conduct towards France, but in which I had no participation; that my correspondence was indeed animated, but if he would condescend to put himself in my position and consider that by his proclamation of neutrality and the interpretation that he had given to it, he had annulled the most sacred treaties, deprived the French people . . . of the alliance which they considered as property dearly bought—he would acknowledge that unless I was a traitor I could not act otherwise."

Genêt then suggested that they discuss a new treaty.

"The President," he stated, "listened to all I had said and simply told me that he did not read the papers, that he did not care what they said concerning his administration"—one occasion, at least, on which Mr. Washington departed from the traditions of the cherry tree. "We left the room, he accompanied me as far as the staircase, took me by the hand and pressed it." The next morning Genêt went to Mr. Jefferson and told him of this inter-

view. Mr. Jefferson blushed—the door opened, and
in walked Mr. Washington. Genêt was not invited
to remain, nor could he ever find out from Mr. Jefferson whether the President had referred to his
nocturnal visit. A few days later, Genêt was called
to New York.

13

Mr. Jefferson was alarmed. He was getting the
worst of it in his perpetual quarrel with Mr. Hamilton; the constant uproar over Genêt was turning
even the Republicans against their party, and consequently against himself. And then this young
man who had made a fool of him before the Cabinet
over the *Petit Démocrate;* who visited the President
without permission, and was liable to tell him Heaven
knew what about his Secretary of State's private
chicaneries—something must be done.

"Never, in my opinion," Mr. Jefferson wrote to
Mr. Madison in July, "was so calamitous an appointment made as that of the present Minister of
France here. Hot headed, all imagination, no
judgment, passionate, disrespectful, and even in-
decent towards the President in his written as well
as his verbal communications"—

a statement directly opposed to Mr. Jefferson's own
testimony in his personal diary.

"I believe," he wrote again a little later, "it will
be true wisdom in the Republican party to approve
unequivocally of a state of neutrality . . . *to
abandon Genêt entirely.* . . . In this way we shall
keep the people on our side by keeping ourselves in

the right.   I have been myself under a cruel dilemna
with him.   I adhered to him as long as I could have
a hope of setting him right"—by encouraging him
in every way, no doubt.   "Finding at length that
the man was incorrigible, I saw the necessity of
quitting a wreck which would but sink all who should
cling to it."

The rats were leaving the sinking ship.   As Mr.
Oliver Wolcott expressed it, Mr. Jefferson "stimu-
lated the prejudices of the French Minister against
his colleagues in the American Cabinet, and, after
he had been seduced into intemperate measures, this
too sanguine instrument of his intriguing ambition
was sacrificed without scruple."

On the evening of his interview with Genêt concerning the brig, Mr. Jefferson stopped in at Governor Mifflin's to report his imagined success, and
found Mr. Dallas there.   They compared their interviews, and, in his diary, Mr. Jefferson recorded that
Mr. Dallas mentioned some things which Genêt had
not said in the second interview, "and particularly
his declaration that he would appeal from the President to the people."   This important and, if au-
thentic, unpardonable threat on the part of a foreign
Minister was repeated by Mr. Jefferson to the Cabinet.   Governor Mifflin also carried it to General
Knox—who imparted it to Mr. Hamilton—as having
been reported to him by his Secretary on the occasion of the first interview.   One may not, lacking
further evidence, presume that these gentlemen acted
otherwise than in good faith and according to their
sincere recollection of a verbal communication.

At all events, Mr. Hamilton notified Mr. Jay and Mr. King of Genêt's alleged indiscretion, and authorized them to publish it. Genêt, arriving at New York on August 7 in the midst of the customary guns and bells, went from the New Coffee House to his lodgings on Maiden Lane and found the "certificate" in the *Diary*. Genêt immediately denied the accusation flatly. Mr. Hamilton and General Knox issued a statement corroborating Mr. Jay and Mr. King, and announcing that their authorities were Governor Mifflin and Mr. Jefferson. Genêt appealed, fruitlessly, to Mr. Washington—"I dare therefore to venture to expect from you an explicit denial, a statement that I have never intimated to you an intention of appealing to the people." Mr. Jefferson replied that the President did not think it necessary to testify against a declaration which, whether made to him or to others, was perhaps immaterial. Genêt characterized this reply as "evasive," and wrote to his Government—

"Knox and Hamilton, alarmed by the tremendous popularity which I enjoy, are spreading the news everywhere that I want to incite the Americans against their government, and that, displeased with its conduct, I have determined to appeal to the people; and this weak government which is always afraid of England deserves such an appeal . . . but since the fact is false I have just written a very firm letter to General Washington."

The question was become one of national controversy. Throughout the summer, while New York and Philadelphia were in the throes of a violent

epidemic of yellow plague—caused, many people
thought, by the godless action of erecting a new
theater at Philadelphia—war raged in the newspapers over Genêt's reported appeal. It was an
outrage, in keeping with similar outrages perpetrated
by his minions and hirelings—it was a base libel, a
Federalist plot to ruin him.   Mr. Monroe concurred
in the latter opinion.

"The monarchy party among us," he wrote, "has
seized a new ground whereon to advance their fortunes.   The French Minister has been guilty in the
vehemence of his zeal of some indiscretions, slighting
the President of the United States, and instead of
healing the breach, this party have brought it to the
public view, and are laboring to turn the popularity
of this respectable citizen against the French Revolution. . . ."

And a little later he told Mr. Jefferson—

"that the object of this party is to separate us from
France and ultimately unite us with England is what
I am well assured of—and that the certificate of
Messrs. Jay and King was concerted at Philadelphia
as the means of bringing the subject before the
public is likewise what I believe. . . .   I consider
the whole however as a mere trick, and which will
ultimately recoil on the authors of it."

Mr. Jefferson who, with his fellow Republican,
Governor Mifflin, had started the rumor, and who
was only too pleased at the prospect of trouble for
the Federalists, and who did not give two pins for

Genêt any more, probably laughed very heartily. Governor Mifflin, for his part, was not so sure now as to just what Mr. Dallas had said, or as to what he himself had said Mr. Dallas had said. Mr. King and Mr. Jay, on their side, were not laughing at all. The Senator from New York and the Chief Justice of the United States did not relish being called liars in the public gazettes; nor did they appreciate the comedy at Philadelphia, where Mr. Hamilton was pointing to General Knox, and General Knox to Governor Mifflin, and Governor Mifflin to Mr. Dallas, and all of them to Mr. Jefferson.

"I find," Mr. Monroe advised him on December 4, "the establishment of the charge against Mr. Genêt will depend principally upon what you heard Mr. Dallas say. This latter will deny that he ever said anything like what the certificate states; Jay and King heard it from Hamilton and Knox, these latter from Mifflin, and I am told that there is a difference between those gentlemen and Mifflin, and likewise between him and Dallas, as to what they respectively stated. So the fact will be disproved against them unless the circumstances they are able to adduce are supported by you."

But Mr. Jefferson said nothing at all, and on December 7, Mr. Dallas issued an official denial of the statement attributed to him. He set forth all that Genêt had said in the interview with regard to the sovereignty of Congress in the matter of the treaties, and the consequent duty of the President to convene Congress to discuss them, and then he announced that—

"Such was Mr. Genêt's conversation with me, and it will be allowed that although I am responsible for the fidelity of the recital I am not responsible for any inference which has been drawn from the facts that it contains."

Then—after admitting that Governor Mifflin might be correct in saying that he, Dallas, had stated that—

"*if after the business was laid before Congress* Mr. Genêt did not receive satisfaction on behalf of his nation, he would publish his appeal, withdraw and leave the governments themselves to settle the dispute"—

Mr. Dallas went on to explain that he was given to understand that Mr. Jefferson had stated—

". . . in an official memorandum, that Mr. Genêt's declaration of an intention to appeal from the President to the people was not expressed to *him*, but to me. Whether Mr. Jefferson employed the language of his own inference from my recital on the occasion, or adopted the language of the current rumor, I will not attempt to discuss.

"But if, in the same early stage of the business, I had also enjoyed the same means of explanation, I, like Mr. Jefferson, should then have said what I said the moment I heard the suggestion applied to *me*, what I have since taken every opportunity of saying, and what I now most solemnly say, that Mr. Genêt never did in conversation with me declare 'that he would appeal from the President to the people,' or that he would make any other appeal which conveyed to mind the idea of exciting insurrection and tumult.

"Upon the whole, as my communications to the Governor and Mr. Jefferson were of an official and confidential nature, I think that I have cause to complain; and the candor of others will induce them to lament *that I was not personally consulted* (which common courtesy as well as common caution might have dictated) before Mr. Hamilton and Mr. Knox (who had daily opportunities of seeing me) undertook to propagate the report connected with my name; or, at least, before Mr. Jay and Mr. King undertook to vouch for its authority."

Very unpleasant reading, one would imagine, for Mr. Jay and Mr. King, for Mr. Hamilton and General Knox, for Governor Mifflin, and for Mr. Jefferson. One almost begins to wonder whether Governor Mifflin did not repeat, and Mr. Jefferson— inadvertently, no doubt—record in his diary, garbled versions of their conversations with Mr. Dallas concerning the young man who was becoming such a menace to the Republican party; and whether Mr. Hamilton and General Knox did not incautiously seize upon them, doubtless in the best of faith, for the purpose of discrediting Genêt, that troublesome pebble in the Federalist shoe. "It is to be regretted," Mr. Jay remarked to Mr. King, "that Mr. Jefferson and Governor Mifflin still remain, as it were, in a back ground."

And for Genêt the situation was not only regrettable, it was fatal. Whatever the facts of the case, the mere repetition of the scandal was capable of destroying him and his cause. Already addresses of loyalty to the President were pouring in from every quarter; from Charleston, Governor Moultrie wrote to Genêt to tell him that he was ruined; he was being spoken of as "too abhorred a villain to have his name mentioned by any man of the least honor or virtue." Between them, and from quite different motives, Mr. Jefferson and Mr. Hamilton had done for him. And this time, in the face of disaster, Genêt quite lost his head. He demanded that Mr. Jay and Mr. King be prosecuted for libel by the Attorney General. Mr. Jefferson transmitted the plea with a request that it be given every consideration, as concerning "a public character peculiarly entitled to the protection of the laws"— why "peculiarly" is not so clear, unless Mr. Jefferson had it in mind that the suit would damage Mr. Hamilton; Mr. Randolph refused to inaugurate proceedings; and Genêt exclaimed that he would "cover himself with the mantle of mourning and say that America is no longer free."

Whereupon, with the advice of Mr. Edward Livingston, he determined to—

"prosecute in your courts of Judicature the authors and abettors of the odious and vile machinations that have been plotted against me by means of a series of impostures which for a while have fascinated the minds of the public, and misled even your First Magistrate. . . ."

14

But that was not all. Troubles were accumulating, both at home and in America, and the disaster was complete. For in August, already, the Cabinet had decided to ask for Genêt's recall, and Mr. Jefferson had written to Mr. Gouverneur Morris, at Paris, to present this request concerning the Minister who had "developed a character and conduct so unexpected and so extraordinary as to place us in the most distressing dilemna." Just how distressing, none but Mr. Jefferson himself was in a position to appreciate. Genêt was officially informed of this step on September 15, and had some interesting observations to make in his reply to Mr. Jefferson, in which he summed up his attitude towards the whole controversy.

"Sir," he told him, "persuaded that the sovereignty of the United States resides essentially in the People and its representation in the Congress; persuaded that the executive power is the only one which has been confided to the President of the United States; persuaded that this Magistrate has not the right to decide questions the discussion of which the Constitution reserves particularly to the Congress; persuaded that he has not the power to bend existing treaties to circumstances and to change their sense . . . I had deferred . . . communicating to my government . . . the original correspondence which has taken place in writing between you and myself on the political rights of France in particular . . . and on the acts, proclamations and decisions of the President of the United States relative to objects which require from their nature the sanction of the legislative body.
"However, informed that the gentlemen who have been painted to me so often"—by whom, one wonders—"as aristocrats, partisans of monarchy, partisans of England . . . were laboring to ruin me

in my country after having reunited all their efforts
to calumniate me in the view of their fellow citizens,
I was going to . . . transmit them to France with
my reports, when the denunciation which those
same men have excited the President to exhibit
against me, through Mr. Morris, came to my hands.
. . .

"It is in the name of the French People that I am
sent to their brethren. . . . It is, then, for the
representatives of the American People, and not
for a single man, to exhibit against me an act of
accusation if I have merited it. . . ."

And so, for perhaps the thousandth time, Genêt
asked, in conclusion, that all the points at issue be
laid before *Congress*.

And in France the Girondists had fallen, the Jacobin Reign of Terror was under way; already in July,
Robespierre's colleagues had been examining the
reported activities of the Minister whose appointment had so angered them, in preparation for a
written rebuke which he must have received some-
time in that same fatal September, and the tone of
which few Envoys, probably, have ever been subjected to by their Government.

"You thought," they informed him, with a convenient disregard of the spirit of his instructions, if
not actually the letter, "that it was your duty to
direct the political affairs of that people and to
persuade it to make common cause with us. . . .
You took it upon yourself to arm privateers, to order
recruiting at Charleston, to cause prizes to be condemned before having been recognized by the American Government . . . and with the certainty of

its disapproval. . . .   Your instructions are directly opposed to this curious interpretation.   You
were ordered to treat with the Government and not
with a portion of the people, to be the representative
of the French Republic at the Congress and not the
chief of an American party. . . .   We may not,
we can not recognize in America any lawful authority
except that of the President and of the Congress.
It is there that the general will of the people resides
without exception."

Precisely, in the Congress—Genêt had been saying
that for months!

"It seems, Citizen," they continued, "that since
your arrival at Charleston, you have been surrounded by very unintelligent, or extremely ill
intentioned people. . . .   They were not aware,
doubtless, that the American Government . . . has
never ceased to make us substantial advances to
furnish us with supplies . . . . and that we have
always found in it the most friendly attitude, joined
to that wise and even timid policy which . . .
especially characterizes General Washington. . . .
Dazzled by a false popularity you have estranged
the only man who should be the spokesman for you
of the American people"—the French Government
had not sat, recently, at the feet of Mr. Jefferson.
"It is not through the effervescence of an indiscreet
zeal that one may succeed with a cold and calculating
people. . . .
"Do not delude yourself any longer concerning the
brilliance of a false popularity which removes from
you the representatives of the people without whom
it will be impossible to bring to a successful close the
negotiations with which you are charged.   Apply

yourself to gaining the confidence of the President and of the Congress; avoid . . . the perfidious insinuations of those who wish to mislead you, and be persuaded especially that it is by reason and not by enthusiasm that you will be able to exercise influence on a people which, even when it was making war on its tyrants, never ceased to remain cold."

One hopes that Genêt sent a copy of this letter to Mr. Jefferson, and to the Democratic Societies of Charleston and Philadelphia.

15

The general will of the people resided in the Congress, so they said, and it was to Congress that Genêt looked for his salvation, to Congress that he had always looked.

"Our friends will sustain us with enthusiasm in defending our rights in the next Congress," he wrote back to France, "disregarding General Washington who sacrifices them to our enemies, and who will never forgive me for having received from his people a support great enough to cause the execution of our treaties in spite of him. . . . The people are for us, and their opinion differs greatly from that of their government."

When Congress met, in December, Mr. Jefferson sent three Senators to see Genêt and effect a reconciliation—for what purpose is not so manifest—but Genêt declined and waited for Congress to express itself. It did so by agreeing to Mr. Washington's condemnation "of a person who has so little respected the mutual dispositions" of France and America. The "appeal to the people" had done its work.

"Congress has met!" Genêt exclaimed, a trifle hysterically, but it was a black moment for him. "Washington has unmasked himself, America is befouled!"

Genêt's successor, Citizen Fauchet—whom Mr. Hamilton described as a meteor following a comet— arrived in January, 1794, and presented himself to Mr. Randolph, now Secretary of State in place of Mr. Jefferson who was indulging in one of his sabbatical periods. Citizen Fauchet brought with him a decree of the Committee of Public Safety disavowing the "criminal conduct" of Genêt, disarming all his privateers, revoking all his Consuls, and requesting his own arrest. Genêt was actually to have been executed aboard the fleet at Brest, without trial. The decree was signed by Barère, Hérault, Billaud-Varennes, Collot d'Herbois, Saint-Just and Robespierre—sinister names at the foot of any document.

Mr. Washington, who had demanded his recall but not his punishment, magnanimously refused to permit the extradition of Genêt. But Mr. Randolph, "your friend," Genêt afterwards wrote to Mr. Jefferson,

"the man of precious confessions, added in confidence that I still had many friends; that it was necessary to wait; but that if France persisted they would examine if the power of the President, which on this point was questionable, might not still afford some expedient to do what France desired."

One would hesitate to believe this if it were not corroborated by Citizen Fauchet himself.

There was nothing left to do except to take over Genêt's enormous files of correspondence, the sorting of which took nearly two weeks, and to examine his accounts which showed that the French government still owed him nine thousand francs, which he was to try and collect, in vain, a good many years later. As for his libel suit against Mr. Jay and Mr. King, Citizen Fauchet reminded him that the family of an Envoy could be held responsible with their lives for his conduct, and suggested that the suit be dropped. One would like to know at whose request.

From Charleston, on March 23, Mr. de Mangourit, his friend, wrote to him—

"I have received, Citizen, the circular in which you announce to me your recall. Since the Republic can only replace one virtuous man with another I console myself.

"The Convention, also, will not see the good which you have done without rendering you a consoling justice; there you will expose the picture of political lies; this treacherous and hideous ingratitude will astonish the incorruptible Robespierre. . . . That Frenchman will be the first to give you the civic kiss."

Mr. de Mangourit, of course, did not have the slightest idea what he was talking about.

"Without you, the liberty of the United States would have perished, her treaties with France would have been torn up, and the British Leopard would have appeared a second time in America. . . .

"Adieu, Genêt!"

16

Adieu, Genêt. . . .

He was thirty-one years old; his career was ended; behind him lay proscription and the scaffold, before him exile. The sale of his furniture, and of his carriage and horses, brought him just enough to buy a small farm, at Jamaica on Long Island. The Citizen Minister became the citizen farmer.

"All these infamies," he wrote to Mr. Jefferson a few years later, referring to the closing episodes of his official life, "have fully justified in the tribunal of my conscience the course I have taken . . . to remain in America after rendering my accounts and placing my papers in the hands of my successor in an honorable manner; and although with little fortune to bury myself in retirement and silence; to meditate upon the great revolutions of the world; to try to penetrate the secrets of nature; and above all to isolate myself from the intrigues of courts and the discouraging cabals of the people."

And then all his resentment against the man who had done so much to ruin him, and against the whole American influence on France, came out in an astonishing paragraph.

"I would to God, Sir," he exclaimed, "that doing more justice to your talents, you had likewise consecrated to the cultivation of the sciences the balance of your life, after having labored in establishing the independence of the United States. I wish that all the other envoys of the Federal government had done the same. France would then perhaps have passed without any suspended motion from one energetic government to another. The blood of the Bourbons, banished like that of the Tarquins, would not have flowed upon the scaffold; the French people, powerful and formidable, would have restrained Europe and found allies . . . and the United States, having conducted themselves strictly as an association of industrious merchants and peaceable farmers who prefer the horn of plenty to the triumph of fame, would not have drawn upon themselves the resentment of all parties who have succeeded each other in France, and who have been all equally deceived. . . ."

But Genêt was not entirely alone at Jamaica. All during the trying months of his final conflict with the Government, and afterwards, while he was gathering together the odds and ends of his life for a fresh start, there was a young lady at New York who saw in him not the Citizen Minister, or the citizen farmer, but just the citizen lover. It was really to see her, probably, that he went to New York on July 4, 1794, and marched with the officials of the state in a long procession of French sympathizers, singing republican songs, and, if one is to believe Mr. de Saint-Méry, hurling insults at the royalist émigrés on the sidewalk. And even here the Federalists tried to interfere, saying that he already had a wife in France; but the wedding finally took place, at Government House, on the evening of Thursday, November 6—

"by the Rev. Dr. Rodgers, Citizen Edmond Charles Genêt, late Minister from the Republic of France, to

Miss Cornelia Tappen Clinton, daughter of His Excellency George Clinton Esquire, Governor of this State."

Miss Cornelia Clinton was twenty years old, a young lady of consequence and great social position.

"Honest, faithful and sincere, she cheerfully retired with the man who had won her hand from the agitated scene of the world to the shades of a peaceful solitude."

One seems, somehow, to learn more about Genêt from those few, simple facts, than from a multitude of official records. Three of their children were born at Jamaica; three others at Prospect Hill, near the village of Greenbush opposite Albany, to which they moved in 1800. She died on March 23, 1810, aged not quite thirty-six, of consumption.

In the meantime, after the fall of Robespierre, Genêt had of course expected to be called back to France. But Mr. Monroe, the new American Minister at Paris, objected, and, in spite of faithful Mr. de Mangourit's exuberant outcries, Genêt's name remained on the list of the proscribed. It was not until several years later that Mr. Monroe finally explained to Genêt the motives for his action.

"As a friend to free government," he told him, "your name will be recorded in the history of the present day, and your patient submission to the censures you incurred, in the station of a frugal and industrious farmer, will be a proof of the uprightness of your heart and integrity of your conduct while a victim to pure principles.

"I considered it a duty not to injure your fame or detract from your merit while I was in France, but to anticipate and prevent as far as I could any ill effects which your collision with our government might produce in the French councils. It was natural, had you returned, that you should have gone into a detail with your government of the incidents attending your mission, and more than probable that the communications you would have made to it would have increased the jealousy which it then entertained of the views of ours. . . . Hence I was persuaded your return at the time might be injurious, and was in fact averse to it. . . .

"The whole of this has passed and is only recollected as interesting to ourselves. I, too, have had my day of suffering. I served with zeal the cause of liberty and my country, and was requited by every injustice which could be rendered me, short of imprisonment and death. This too has passed, though it can never be recollected by me but with disgust."

Napoleon, First Consul, finally invited Genêt to return, but the latter would have nothing to do with a man who was thinking of making himself emperor, and refused. He settled permanently at Prospect Hill, and, with Lieutenant Governor Broome and Mr. De Witt Clinton as sponsors, became a naturalized American citizen—in the presence, so family tradition asserts, of Mr. Alexander Hamilton, who addressed the Supreme Court and expressed the opinion that it was a notable event and a compliment to American institutions.

In a way, Genêt had, at last, appealed to the American people. . . .

17

On July 31, 1814, Genêt, for four years a widower, married Miss Martha Brandon Osgood; a young lady of twenty-seven—daughter of Mr. Samuel Osgood, the first Postmaster General—who gave him five children, and survived him by a good many years.

Genêt himself had still twenty years to live. Noted everywhere for his courtesy, he occupied himself extensively with Democratic politics and prison reform; he was keenly interested in the Erie Canal and other similar projects; he spent much of his time in scientific research, and invented and patented a lifeboat; he wrote many pamphlets on learned subjects—*On the means of opening new sources of wealth for the northern states, On public health and public improvements, On the upward forces of fluids and their applicability to several arts. . . .*

But he was a disappointed man; he never forgave what seemed to him his mother country's injustice to him; he "felt himself so much injured that he almost wished to avoid mankind," his wife told Madame Ney.

"Therefore this place surrounded by woods, at a distance from the metropolis, suited him better than any other. How often have I grieved that his splendid talents should be buried in obscurity."

Perhaps, too, the place surrounded by woods re-minded him of Mainville, and those happy, far-off times with his sisters at Uncle Toto's; perhaps, at

dusk sometimes, he almost heard the echoes of Uncle
Toto's flute, playing *Charming Gabrielle* and *My
Merry Shepherd*—those old tunes—while he thought
of old days, at Versailles in the little white suits, at
St. Petersburg in the handsome uniform of Dragoons,
at Charleston on the quarterdeck of the *Embuscade*,
at Oeller's Tavern at Philadelphia. Such different
days, for now they were very poor—there were law-
suits and mortgages—and this old gentleman of
sixty-nine was obliged to write to his niece in France,
in 1832—

"To tell you the truth, honors without emoluments
would not soften my distress.   If it was not thought
proper to reinstate me here as Minister, I would
consent to accept the post of Consul General . . .
or even that of mere Consul at New York."

Mere Consul at New York. . . .
He died, at Prospect Hill, on July 14, 1834.   They
buried him at Greenbush, where—

"Under this humble stone, are interred the remains
of Edmond Charles Genêt, late Adjutant General,
Minister Plenipotentiary and Consul General from
the French Republic to the United States of America.
He was born at Versailles, Parish of St. Louis, in
France, January 8, 1763, and died at Prospect Hill,
Town of Greenbush, July 14, 1834.
"Driven by the storms of the Revolution to the
shades of retirement, he devoted his talents to his
Adopted Country, where he cherished the love of
liberty and virtue.   The pursuits of literature and
science enlivened his peaceful solitude, and he
devoted his life to usefulness and benevolence.   His

last moments were like his life, an example of fortitude and true Christian philosophy.   His heart was
love and friendship's sun, which has set on this
Transitory World to rise with radiant splendor
beyond the grave."

Adieu, Genêt. . . .